monday morning

Editing

By Murray Suid, Wanda Lincoln and Maryann Gatheral
Illustrated by Corbin Hillam

This book is dedicated to:
~~William Shakespeare~~
~~Ray Bradbury~~
~~Judy Blume~~
Our Readers

Publisher: Roberta Suid
Editor: Carol Whiteley
Designer: David Hale

ISBN 0-912107-00-6

Printed in the United States of America

CONTENTS

INTRODUCTION

No one wants to fly with a pilot who can handle takeoffs but not landings. Likewise, people don't enjoy reading a story by someone who's good at composing a first draft but lacks the skills or heart to revise it.

Savvy writers agree that *editing* is the key to creativity and competence. This is true whether the finished product is a poem, a bumpersticker, a book review, a business letter, an essay, a novel, or any other kind of writing.

Unfortunately, few students know the joy of turning an awkward draft into a polished manuscript. Most view editing as a cruel and unusual chore. Fearing that a crossed-out word is a sign of ignorance, novice writers prefer to turn in unmarked — and usually unremarkable — papers of little interest to anyone including themselves.

But this is not the inevitable scenario. Kids *can* learn to edit. They can even learn to *love* editing, which indeed is a universal skill valued by scientists, cooks, musicians, carpenters, football players, astronauts, and everyone else who's got the "right stuff."

Pages 6-7 provide a bird's-eye view of a classroom featuring activities and materials that teach the true nature and significance of editing. Look closely and you'll see:

- **bulletin boards** that a) relate editing to the overall writing process and b) present edited manuscripts by famous writers;
- **an editing center** fitted out with dictionaries, thesauruses, almanacs, colored pencils, tape, scissors, a word processor, and other helpful materials;
- **peer editing groups** of the sort many journalists, poets, ad writers, and authors rely on.

This book outlines two strategies for helping you develop this kind of classroom.

Strategy 1. Teach the basic editing skills using non-threatening "simulated" first drafts.

Boil down editing and you get critical reading. The writer-as-editor slowly, carefully reviews a text with one main question in mind: "How can I make it better?" *Better* equals *clearer* and *more interesting*.

Students rarely get the chance to practice this activity because almost everything they read has previously been edited. It's a rare youngster who can spot ways to improve professionally produced novels, textbooks, newspaper articles, advertisements, and so on.

Of course, students *could* develop editing skills by trying to revise their own work. The trouble is that such material is notoriously difficult to deal with: there are often so many problems mixed together in so confusing a muddle that even an expert would be baffled. On top of that, editing one's own manuscript is trickier and more painful than probing someone else's efforts.

For these reasons — and others soon to be apparent — you'll do better to use simulated first drafts for introducing and honing editing skills.

The easiest and yet most powerful way to do this is with the **Daily Edit** activity, a chalkboard exercise requiring five minutes or less at the start of each class period. Though simple in concept, this technique has brought about remarkable reading and writing gains in hundreds of classrooms throughout the U.S. and Canada. For specific implementation suggestions, see the next section of this book.

Forty duplicatable **worksheets,** which comprise the center portion of this book, offer a more in-depth editing experience. These handouts systematically explore the ten basic editing skills:

- taking stock of a manuscript
- cutting what's not needed
- adding missing material
- improving the order
- checking facts
- improving word choice
- improving sentences
- catching spelling mistakes
- checking the punctuation
- preparing the final manuscript

Each skill is introduced by a **lesson** containing background information, activities, games, and projects.

The duplicatable worksheets prepare students for "real world" editing in two ways. First, they teach the standard editing marks used to indicate inserts ($\wedge$), deletions ($\mathscr{D}$), capitalization changes ($\cancel{X}=a$), new paragraphs ($\P$), and so on. Second, the handouts present a wide variety of authentic-looking texts: book reviews, letters, bumperstickers, product labels, vanity license plates, newspaper headlines, and even error-

filled fortune cookie fortunes. The find-the-mistake-in-the-picture lessons offer editing experiences for even the young child.

Many of the worksheets ask for specific answers. These are given in the **answer section.**

Note: In no way do the worksheets provide an exhaustive set of editing experiences. Use them as models for creating your own tailor-made simulations. For example, if your students need more picture edits, arrange for a high-school art class to supply you with dozens of error-filled illustrations. If you want your students to have more practice editing business letters, write some yourself or enlist the aid of a typing class.

There are two other ways you can provide your class with non-threatening editing practice. First, let students know that, like everyone else, you make mistakes

and that you want their editorial help. When students spot a problem in something you've written — on the board or in a handout — accept their comments with the kind of grace you want them to show when they read your suggestions in the margins of their papers.

Second, challenge students to correct mistakes found in newspapers, textbooks, billboards, public signs, store window displays, Chinese fortune cookie fortunes, and other "mass" media. By making a bulletin board display of such bloopers, collected by the teacher and students, you'll provide everyone with opportunities for mental editing.

To squeeze more editing awareness from this material, have students write friendly complaint letters to the authors of the bloopers. These letters might even contain photographs that document the problems.

Strategy 2. Guide students into real editing.

One does not survive by simulation alone. The proof of the practice comes when students begin to edit their own work and that of their peers. The **program** section gives step-by-step suggestions for helping students move from practice to application. This section covers such topics as:

- assessing skills
- demonstrating editing
- creating an editing environment
- guiding students into self-editing
- finding time for teacher-student conferences
- establishing peer-editing groups
- involving parents
- providing more effective feedback while reducing the burden of paper grading

A series of **bulletin boards** and a **resources** section that includes rough drafts by famous authors provide additional encouragement for "real world" editing.

That's about it, except for a last word of caution. Becoming a thoughtful, creative writer/editor is not the work of a day, a week, or a month. So, in addition to stimulating simulations, motivating bulletin boards, parental involvement, and school-wide cooperation, you'll need a little patience.

Make that *a lot* of patience.

Writewell Elementary School
1111 Woodgreen Avenue
Literacy, California 94301

Don Dunker, Owner
Dons Donuts
530 University A
Literacy, Califor

Dear Mr. Dunker:

The fifth graders at Writewell Elementary School love your donuts, but we're not so crazy about the name of your shop. Since ownership is indicated by '<u>s</u>, the sign over the front door should read:
Don's Donuts

We're not so concerned for ourselves because our teacher has taught us to mentally edit the words when we walk by. However, we do worry about younger children who may be learning the wrong idea about possessives.

For this reason, we urge you to correct your sign. Thanks for looking into this matter.

Sincerely,
Eddie Torr
Eddie Torr

SKILLS

The Amazing Daily Edit

The Daily Edit activity is so simple in concept — students spending a few minutes at the start of class trying to improve a short passage — that you may have trouble believing it can make a significant difference when the time comes for teaching kids how to edit. But teachers who have experimented with the technique in grades one through twelve report that the process works. See for yourself. Here are several steps to consider:

First, present the text on the board or the overhead projector:

> too heads are better then one

Second, after mentally editing this text, students copy it *correctly* into their special "daily edit" notebooks or regular journals. (Early in the year, to make the task less threatening, you might have your students work in pairs.) The teacher or, better, a student, then edits the material on the board with the help of the audience. Comments should be as specific as possible: not, "Fix the spelling" but rather "Spell the first word T-w-o."

> Two
> ~~too~~ heads are better th~~e~~n one⊙
>   a

The person running the edit (the teacher or, after some practice, the student) should sometimes ask for an explanation —"Why do we need a capital *t*?"— as a way of reinforcing the concepts underlying the editing changes: "It's a capital *t* because a sentence should start with a capital letter."

Indicate changes in the text using standard editing marks (see Resources). Making revisions with colored chalk (or colored pens if using the overhead projector) can add clarity.

Then, have students compare their work with the group-edited version. Final adjustments are to be encouraged.

The key to this program's success is the word *daily*. By trying to improve a piece of writing on a regular basis, students will develop the editing habit. And because the mock drafts are short and generally easy to revise, confidence will grow day by day.

SOURCES OF MOCK DRAFTS. The simplest way to obtain material for the daily edit is to buy it ready-made. A popular example is the series of booklets for grades one through nine sold by D.O.L. Publications, 1001 Kingston Avenue, Racine, WI 53402. One big advantage of purchasing such a program is continuity. The daily edit will go on even if you're absent, and it's easy to implement on a school-wide basis.

The drawbacks of packaged edits are that they tend to be artificial and not related to your students' lives. Also, a ready-made program cannot meet the specific needs of your class. For example, your kids may need less work on missing apostrophes and more work on pronoun references.

This leads us, therefore, to the second source: you! Writing your own daily editing materials not only lets you tailor the exercise to your class but also gives you the opportunity to start the day with a genuine message:

> Today we will go to the
> the Learning Center at 10-30 a.m.

You might also adapt material — a joke, a proverb, a song lyric, a tongue twister, a few lines from a novel or a poem, a newspaper headline, a paragraph from a science article, a startling fact from *The Guinness Book of Records*, a bumpersticker, an excerpt from a textbook, or a famous saying. Adapting allows you to introduce students to a wide variety of literary forms and authors.

If you choose to write your own daily edits, pages 14-15, Model Mock Edits, can serve as a starting point for deciding what editing problems to include. In the models, all sentences require beginning and ending punctuation, since most students need continual practice in these areas.

Notice that one of the items has *no* overt problem. By presenting an O.K. draft now and then, you'll be teaching students that in editing, as in life, leaving well enough alone can be a good idea.

Keeping track of the skills you're working on can get a little tricky, especially since you may eventually want to include several problems in a single mock draft. Page 16, Daily Edit Problem Chart, should make the record-keeping task easier for you.

Your students can create some of the daily edits. On Monday, for example, you might assign Eric the job of writing a missing-word edit for use on Tuesday. On Tuesday, ask Wilma to prepare a mock draft that requires her peers to distinguish between *it's* and *its*.

But why, you might wonder, should students write daily edit material? The answer is simple. Deliberately — as opposed to mindlessly — making a mistake requires one to think carefully about the problem. Prove it to yourself by creating your own example.

No matter who writes the daily edits — teacher or students or both — be sure to keep the material reasonably simple. Part of the power of this exercise is that it is quick and non-traumatic.

A VARIATION. There is, however, one variation that is worth trying occasionally. We call it the "you-take-the-criticism" edit. It looks just like the regular mock edit only this time there's an editor's note in the margin:

There's more than one way skin a cat.   *Word Missing*

This kind of "simulated" comment can help prepare students for accepting and responding to actual criticism from the teacher or from a classmate. When students produce such mock drafts, they are also getting practice in playing the role of the helpful editor.

Model Mock Edits

missing word	rome wasn't built in day	Rome wasn't built in a day
extra word	mighty oaks from little little acorns grow	Mighty oaks from ~~little~~ little acorns grow
misplaced word	the leopard can't change spots his	The leopard can't change spots his
vague word	if you play with fire, you might get hurt	If you play with fire you might get burned ~~hurt~~
wrong word	let sleeping dogs lay	Let sleeping dogs lie ~~lay~~
spelling — basic error	the cameleon does not leave one tree until he's sure of another	The chameleon does not leave one tree until he's sure of another
spelling — homonyms	a small whole can sink a big ship	A small hole ~~whole~~ can sink a big ship
spelling — look-alikes	birds off a feather flock together	Birds of ~~off~~ a feather flock together
spelling — apostrophe	you cant judge a book by it's cover	You can't judge a book by its cover
spelling — capitalization	when in rome, do as the romans do	When in Rome, do as the Romans do
spelling — missing space	still water runsdeep	Still water runs deep
spelling — extra space	if you walk on snow, you can't hide your foot prints	If you walk on snow, you can't hide your footprints
spelling — plurals	use honey to catch flys	Use honey to catch flies ~~flys~~

14

Model Mock Edits

punctuation — missing comma	if the shoe fits wear it	If the shoe fits, wear it.
punctuation — misplaced comma	"drop by drop fills the tub", she said	"Drop by drop fills the tub," she said.
punctuation — extra comma	a stitch in time, saves nine	A stitch in time saves nine.
punctuation — missing question mark	if you have eaten the morsel on Wednesday, why look for it on Thursday	If you have eaten the morsel on Wednesday, why look for it on Thursday?
punctuation — missing quotes	he who cannot dance will say, The drum is bad	He who cannot dance will say, "The drum is bad."
punctuation — wrong mark	an empty sack cannot stand up?	An empty sack cannot stand up.
grammar — subject-verb	all sunshine make a desert	All sunshine makes a desert.
grammar — pronoun reference	a chain is only as strong as their weakest link	A chain is only as strong as its weakest link.
grammar — run-on sentence	measure your cloth ten times you can cut it only once	Measure your cloth ten times. You can cut it only once.
factual error	the leopard can't change his stripes	The leopard can't change his spots.
logic error	if you walk on snow, you can hide your footprints	If you walk on snow, you can't hide your footprints.
no problem	Talk does not cook rice.	Talk does not cook rice.

Daily Edit Problem Chart

DATE																							
PROBLEM																							

PROBLEM

- missing word
- extra word
- misplaced word
- vague word
- wrong word
- sp.-basic error
- sp.-homonyms
- sp.- look-alikes
- sp.-apostrophe
- sp.- capitalization
- sp.-missing space
- sp.-extra space
- sp.- plurals
- punc.-missing comma
- punc.-misplaced comma
- punc. - extra comma
- punc.- missing question mark
- punc.- missing quotes
- punc.- wrong mark
- grammar - subject-verb
- grammar- pronoun reference
- grammar- run-on sentence
- factual error
- logic error
- no problem

Taking Stock

- understanding what a first draft is
- learning to spot strengths and weaknesses in a manuscript

In some ways an editor is like a doctor who, before prescribing a remedy, needs to get an overall picture of the patient. The following activities are meant to help students understand how this crucial step works when it comes to writing.

ASSESSING THE STRENGTHS AND WEAKNESSES OF A PICTURE. *Worksheet 1,* What's Good and What Could Be Better?, asks students to analyze the good and bad points of a sketch.

LOOKING OVER AN EDITOR'S SHOULDER. *Worksheet 2,* Making Changes in a Piece of Writing, gives students the chance to examine an edited manuscript. By answering a series of questions about the work, students should begin to see the richness of the editing process. This particular activity should be repeated frequently with other marked-up drafts produced by the teacher or by the students.

LITERARY DISCUSSIONS. The skills of "taking stock" get a workout whenever students discuss a story, poem, or essay. This activity is as important in first grade as it is in graduate school.

A good way to do this is for the teacher to read the work out loud. Ask the students to brainstorm titles for it. Then discuss what was good about the story and how it could have been better.

If possible, use examples by students as well as professionals but make sure the student authors are anonymous. Use student writing from past years.

What's Good and What Could Be Better?

Whenever you make anything, you need to spend some time looking at it. When you do this, you should ask yourself two important questions: "What's good about my work?" and "How can I make it better?"

Try it here. Imagine that you are building a new amusement park. At the moment it looks like the picture on this page. Study the picture. Then, underneath it, list what's good about it and what changes would make it better.

What's good?   What changes would make it better?

Making Changes in a Piece of Writing

The job of writing isn't finished after you've put words on paper. You need to look over your work and see what changes might make it better. That's what the writer of the following story did. Read the story and then answer the questions below.

How Did Superman Get His Start?

1)   In ~~1935~~ *1933*, two high school boys named *Jerry* Siegel and *Joe* Schuster got the idea for

2)   a comic book hero. Siegel wrote the words of the story and Schuster drew

3)   the pictures. When the work was done, Superman was born.

4)   Excited about ~~there~~ *their* work, the two boys mailed the comic to ~~to~~ a company

5)   that published comic books. The people at the company said that the story

6)   wasn't good enough. They sent ~~the story~~ *it* back.

7)   The boys tried another company. The same thing happened. Then it

8)   happened again and again. Only after ~~six~~ *five* years did a publishing com-

9)   pany take the story. The first *S*uperman comic came out in ~~1939~~ *1938*. Within

10) (weeks) a few ∧ Superman became one ~~off~~ *of* the most popular heroes ever.

Questions

1. In which line was a repeated word crossed out? _____

2. In which lines were number facts changed? _____

3. Which spelling mistakes were corrected? _____

4. In which line was a word moved so the sentence would make more sense? _____

5. In which line does one new word replace two other words? _____

6. In which line was a lowercase letter changed into a capital letter? _____

7. In which line were missing words added? _____

Cutting What's Not Needed

- removing irrelevant material
- removing redundant material

Crossing out words that one has struggled to put onto paper is not easy. It takes a kind of hardheartedness that is gained slowly. This is certainly one skill that is best practiced on someone else's material.

CUTTING DETAILS FROM A PICTURE. *Worksheet 3, Extra! Extra! Do Something About It!*, asks students to list cuts that should be made in a drawing that's filled with redundant and irrelevant details.

CUTTING EXTRA WORDS FROM SENTENCES. *Worksheet 4*, Cutting Extra Words, extends the activity into the verbal arena. Students also get practice in using the omit symbol.

To dramatize the cutting process while having some fun, create a short sentence that has an extra word or two. Write each word on a large card. Have a group of students hold up the cards in the right order at the front of the room. The audience will act as editor in deciding which card-carrying student or students should sit down.

CUTTING IRRELEVANT SENTENCES. The next step is learning to spot extra ideas in context. *Worksheet 5*, Cutting Sentences That Don't Belong, has students removing sentences from short, non-fiction essays. Once again, this is an activity that could be acted out by students at the front of the room.

Worksheet 6, Cutting Extra Steps, calls for removing steps that don't belong in sets of directions.

Extra! Extra! Do Something About It!

In the picture below you'll find extra words or objects. Your job is to tell the artist which of those extras should be cut out. Write the changes that should be made in the space under the picture.

Cutting Extra Words

1. The following sentences tell about unusual laws. Cross out the extra word or words in each sentence using the mark: (⁄). A sample has been done for you.

A. In North Carolina, a law says that you cannot sing ~~sing~~ out of tune.

B. Frog-jumping contests are against the the law in in Boston nightclubs.

C. In Kentucky a man is not allowed to marry his wife's grandmother in Kentucky.

D. In the state of Maine, you are not permitted permitted to set fire to a mule.

E. While a mule might kick a person in Arizona, the the law says that a person may not kick a mule.

F. It is illegal in New York to pawn a the flag.

G. You'll will need a hunting license to trap a mouse in California.

H. In San Francisco, when you want to take your elephant for a a walk, it the elephant must be kept on on a leash.

I. According to the a law, tomatoes may not be put into clam clam chowder in Massachusetts.

2. Now write a sentence with extra words and see if a friend can find and cut them out.

Cutting Sentences That Don't Belong

The following paragraphs tell about unusual people. Each paragraph contains one sentence that does not belong. Your job is to cut that sentence by drawing this kind of a line through it: ——————

A. "First Names"

If you sometimes wish you had a different first name, think about this one: *Truewillaughing- lifebuckyboomermanifestdestiny.* That's the real first name of a baby born in Florida. Florida is famous for its oranges. The baby even has two middle names: George James.

B. "Boxing Champion"

Though you won't find her name in any record book, Hessie Donahue was once heavyweight boxing champion of the world. Many people enjoy going to boxing matches. Hessie knocked out John L. Sullivan, who was the heavyweight champion of the time.

C. "Making a Big Splash"

Fred Garcia III is a record-breaking swimmer. In 1977 he passed the Red Cross beginner's water safety test. This happened in June. Amazingly, Fred was only eight months old at the time.

D. "A Better Beanstalk"

If they ever make a movie about Jack and the Beanstalk, they should get George Willig to play Jack. A few years ago Willig climbed up the outside of New York's World Trade Center office building. There are skyscrapers in many cities. It took him less than four hours to reach the 110th floor, 1,350 feet above the street.

Cutting Extra Steps

1. Cross out one step in each of the following directions. Then renumber the steps.

A. Shooting a Basketball
Step 1. Wash your hands.
Step 2. Get a good grip on the ball.
Step 3. Take aim at the basket.
Step 4. Throw the ball.

B. Writing and Sending a Letter to a Friend
Step 1. Get paper and pencil.
Step 2. Think about the news you want to share.
Step 3. Turn on the radio.
Step 4. Write the letter.
Step 5. Put the letter in an envelope.
Step 6. Address the envelope and put a stamp on it.
Step 7. Mail the letter.

C. Planting Corn
Step 1. Buy the corn seeds.
Step 2. Prepare the soil.
Step 3. Put the seeds in the ground.
Step 4. Cover up the seeds.
Step 5. Plant the radish seeds somewhere else.

D. Getting Dressed in the Morning
Step 1. Pick out the clothes you want to wear.
Step 2. Put the clothes on.
Step 3. Have some breakfast.
Step 4. Check yourself in the mirror.

2. Write a four-or five-step set of directions for an activity. Include an extra step. See if a friend can find and cross out what's not needed.

Adding Missing Material

● filling in missing details

Leaving a hole in a piece of writing is easy to do. *Spotting* a hole — whether a letter, word, phrase, or detail — is trickier. This is because the writer, knowing what's supposed to be there, unconsciously fills the gap. Unfortunately the reader, being more or less in the dark, is often confused or annoyed omissions. (Were you bothered by the missing *by* in the last sentence?)

While spotting and filling holes should be part of the daily edit practice, the following four activities deal with the problem in greater depth.

LOOKING FOR MISSING DETAILS. *Worksheet 7*, What's Missing?, gives students a chance to practice identifying missing details in an illustration.

INSERTING MISSING WORDS. *Worksheet 8*, Missing Words, deals with words omitted from sentences. The exercise introduces the caret (∧), which is the editor's symbol for inserting material.

ADDING MISSING STEPS. *Worksheet 9*, Completing Directions, asks students to catch omissions in several sets of instructions.

ADDING DETAILS. *Worksheet 10*, Adding Details to a Description, has students add a missing sentence to a descriptive paragraph.

What's Missing?

Here's a chance to see how good you are at catching what isn't there. The picture below is missing about 10 details. List those that you find in the space at the bottom of the page. The first one has been done for you.

Bill is missing an l.

Missing Words

It's easy to leave words out when you're writing a first draft. Every writer does that. The trick is being able to read over your work and fill in what's missing.

1. Each of the following sentences is missing a word. The place where the word should go is marked by a sign called a caret. It looks like this: ∧   Wherever you see a caret, write the missing word above it. The first one has been done for you.

A. "I dropped ∧ egg," Tom cracked.
          an

B. "Math ∧ my worst subject," Tom added.

C. "Gee, my feet hurt," Tom ∧ flatly.

D. "I want to win ∧ race," Tom said swiftly.

E. "I like ∧ shoot arrows," Tom said pointedly.

F. "This is ∧ beautiful mountain spring," Tom gushed.

2. Some words have been left out of the following rhyme. Use a caret (∧) to mark where each word should be. Then write a word that makes sense above the caret. The first one has been done for you.

G. Humpty Dumpty sat ∧ a wall,
                on

H. Humpty had great fall.

I. All King's horses and all King's men

J. Had scrambled for breakfast at ten.

3. Write your own sentence with a missing word. See if a classmate can edit the sentence.

Completing Directions

If you leave out a step when you tell someone how to do something, the person will be confused. That's why people who write cookbooks, how-to-do-it books, and other instructions check their writing many times.

1. Each of the following directions is missing one step. Complete the directions by writing the missing step where it belongs. Then renumber the steps. A sample has been done for you.

A. How to Jump Off a High Diving Board

Step 1. Climb the board.
Step 1.² Close your eyes.

Step 2.³ Jump.

B. How to Fry an Egg

Step 1. Melt butter in a pan.

Step 2. When the egg is cooked, remove it.

C. How to Use a Phone

Step 1. Lift up the receiver.

Step 2. Talk.

Step 3. Hang up.

D. How to Use an Instant Camera

Step 1. Put film in the camera.

Step 2. Look for something to take pictures of.

Step 3. Show the pictures to your friends.

Adding Details to a Description

Next to each picture below is a paragraph that describes the picture. Each paragraph is missing one important detail. Study the picture. Then add a sentence to the paragraph.

A.

A capital B is in the center of a triangle. A small m is inside each corner of the triangle.

B.

A triangle is over the line. A circle is under the line.

C.

A larger square sits on top of a smaller square. Inside the larger square is a circle.

D.

A triangle is around a circle. The triangle is inside a square but doesn't touch the square.

Improving Order

- organizing ideas
- editing sentences
- editing directions

"A place for everything and everything in its place." Like a lot of wise sayings, this one is ten times easier said than done. Even highly experienced writers have trouble knowing what comes first, what goes last, and what belongs in the middle. Still, if we make the practices easy enough, children can begin to sharpen their organizational skills.

REORDERING PARTS OF A PICTURE. *Worksheet 11*, Where Does It Belong?, asks students to relocate misplaced items in a picture.

ORDERING EVENTS IN A COMIC. *Worksheet 12*, First Things First, challenges readers to rearrange the panels of a comic-strip story. This can be done by renumbering the panels but, especially with younger children, it makes more sense to cut apart the panels and physically reorder them.

Comics, happily, are an easy-to-get free material and this is an activity you might repeat often using examples clipped from your local newspaper.

REORDERING WORDS IN A SENTENCE. *Worksheet 13*, Word Moving, has students using a standard editing mark to transport misplaced words to their proper locations.

REORDERING SENTENCES. The culminating activity in this unit is relocating sentences. *Worksheet 14*, Tangled Directions, requires renumbering items in a list of directions.

COMPOSITION TIP. Many organizational problems can be avoided if students know their organizational plan *before* writing. With younger students you might assign the plan, that is, require that the story be told in chronological order or that the topics of the essay be presented by rank. Older students can decide on the plan themselves but should articulate it at the top of their papers. For example, a student might put the following sentence at the top of his or her outline: "I'm planning to organize my essay in chronological order," or "I'm going to discuss the chess pieces in a ranking order — from least valuable to most."

Where Does It Belong?

The picture below is filled with things that are not where they are supposed to be. Your job is to tell the artist what changes should be made to make the picture better. Write each change in the space under the picture.

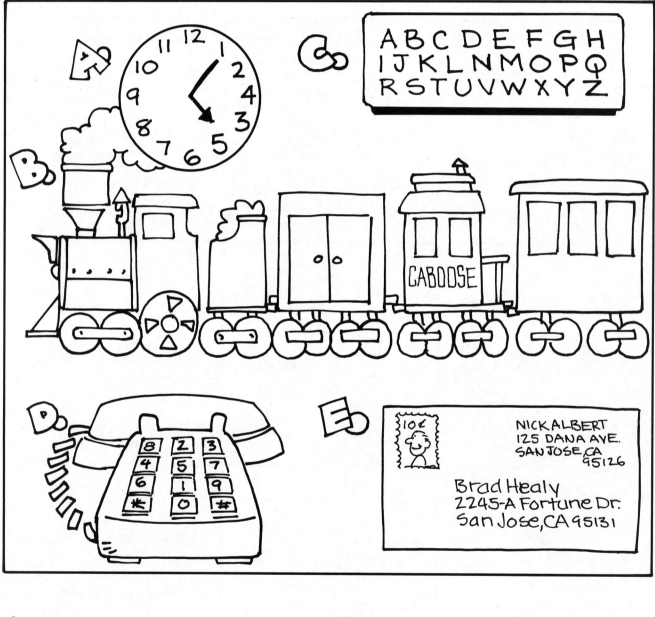

A: _____

B: _____

C: _____

D: _____

E: _____

First Things First

1. The pictures on this page would tell a story except that they are out of order. Your job is to number each picture in an order that makes sense to you. Put the number in the box at the bottom of the picture.

2. Write a story about what happened.

Word Moving

EDITING
FIX-UP
TRUCK

1. The following "cat" fortune cookie fortunes have one or more words that are out of order. Use the editor's mark shown in the example to move the word or words to the right place. Then rewrite the fortune.

Example: Each of your nine lives will happy be.

_____

A. You are going to catch big a mouse.

_____

B. You'll many have happy cat naps.

_____

C. You will a dog chase up a tree.

_____

D. You will star in a TV food cat commercial.

_____

E. Someday you'll turn a lion into.

_____

F. You will never have another flea bite life in your.

_____

G. You will land on always your feet.

_____

H. Your owner mind won't if you scratch the furniture.

_____

Tangled Directions

1. Each of the following directions has a step out of order. Circle the step and use the editor's mark (∩) to show where it belongs. Then renumber the steps.

EDITING FIX-UP TRUCK

Example: Washing Your Hands

Step 1. Rub hands with soap.   Step 1. Rub hands with soap.

Step 2. Wet hands.   Step 2. Wet hands.

Step 3. Dry hands.   Step 3. Dry hands.

A. Making Buttered Toast

Step 1. Put the bread into the toaster.

Step 2. Butter the toast.

Step 3. When the toaster pops, remove the toast.

B. Sharpening a Pencil

Step 1. Turn the handle.

Step 2. Put the pencil into the sharpener.

Step 3. Take the pencil out and check the point.

C. Catching a Fish

Step 1. Drop the hook into the water.

Step 2. Wait until a fish bites.

Step 3. Yank on the line.

Step 4. Pull the fish in.

Step 5. Tie a hook on a line and put a worm on the hook.

2. On the back of this paper, write directions for any activity. Mix up the steps. Then see if a friend can put the steps in the right order.

Checking the Facts

- distinguishing between facts and opinions
- correcting factual errors
- researching

Like a witness at a trial, a writer needs deep respect for the truth. This is as crucial for the fiction writer as for the journalist. After all, labeling Abraham Lincoln the second president of the U.S. would be as outrageous an error in a novel as it would be in a textbook.

To put it directly: Every writer must learn how to recognize and double-check the facts.

CORRECTING VISUAL ERRORS. *Worksheet 15,* What's Wrong Here?, has students identifying mistakes in a city scene. Corrections are made as suggestions to the artist.

SEEKING THE TRUTH. A commitment to truth is one thing; knowing how to find the truth is another. *Worksheet 16,* Finding the Facts, outlines the three basic ways of gathering information — using books and other packaged resources, interviewing experts, and using one's own senses to examine the world firsthand. The handout has students produce facts from each of these sources.

CATCHING TRAVEL-DIRECTION MISTAKES. *Worksheet 17,* Yummytown, presents several sets of directions relating to a simple map. Students catch errors by checking the directions against the "reality" of the map.

What's Wrong Here?

The picture below is filled with mistakes. Your job is to tell the artist at least ten ways to make it better. Write each change in the space under the picture.

Finding the Facts

Each of the following sentences says something that is not true. Your job is to find out what the truth is. You can do this by reading a book, asking someone (but not your teacher), or using your own eyes. When you find an answer, cross out the mistake and write the fact above it. In the space following the sentence, tell where you found the fact.

EDITING
FIX-UP
TRUCK

1. Albert Einstein, the famous scientist, died in 1950. _____

_____

2. The United Nations first met in 1972. _____

_____

3. The Nile River is 2,000 miles long. _____

_____

4. Queen Elizabeth I was born in 1502. _____

_____

5. Cleveland, Ohio, was named for Morton Cleaveland. _____

_____

6. The Spanish flag has two stars on it. _____

_____

7. A worker bee usually lives for one day. _____

_____

8. The Wright brothers' first flight was in July. _____

_____

Yummytown

Circle each error. On another sheet of paper, write the correct directions.

1 To go from the COOKIE shop to the SANDWICH shop:

A. Go north on 2nd Avenue to O street.
B. Turn east.
C. Go to 4th Avenue and you'll be there.

2 How to get from the FISH store to the Doughnut stand:

A. Go east on Q street.
B. When you come to the Taco store turn north. This will be 2nd Avenue.
C. Head north two blocks and you'll be there.

On another piece of paper, make up your directions, including mistakes. See if a friend can fix the directions.

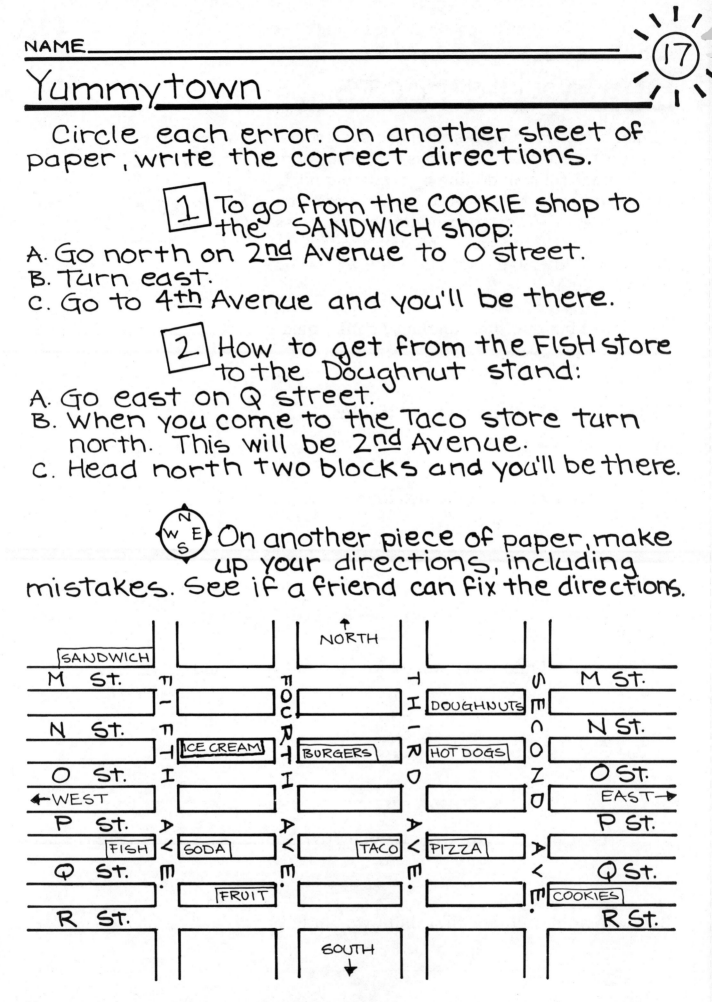

Improving Word Choice

- using precise language
- avoiding mindless repetitions
- developing vocabulary
- avoiding clichés
- using the thesaurus

An old saw has it that there are only three dozen stories to tell. All a writer does is recycle the old ones. Certainly that's what Shakespeare did.

It sounds easy. The hitch is that while picking among 36 plots won't boggle anyone's mind, trying to pick the right word out of the 1,000,000 available is a little trickier. And the thing is, you have to do it again and again and again and...

The key verb to watch in that last paragraph is *pick*. Good writers get to be very choosy about their words. They often report trying out six or eight or more words for a single slot. Perhaps the biggest difference between effective and ineffective writers is the former's patient, persistent, insistent approach to picking words. The following activities aim to give students a sense of this process.

REPLACING TRITE AND VAGUE EXPRESSIONS. *Worksheet 18*, Nice Is Not Nice Enough, has students deleting the word *nice* from a series of bottles, boxes, and other containers. *Worksheet 19*, Don't Always Say *Said*, extends the previous activity into the more literary context of story writing. *Worksheet 20*, Don't Go Wrong with Go, involves replacing *go* with more precise verbs. And though you won't find an instant cure for "Thingitis," *Worksheet 21*,The Thing Problem, can be a beginning.

OVERCOMING WORDINESS. Two heads may be better than one, but the same mathematics doesn't hold when it comes to writing. *Worksheet 22*, One Word Can Be Better Than Two, requires paring down prose to the essentials.

Nice Is Not Nice Enough

Soup can be *nice*. A car can be *nice*. So can clothes. *Nice* is used in so many ways it's hard to know just what it means. No wonder careful writers usually try to replace *nice* with a word that does a better job telling what a thing looks like, sounds like, feels like, tastes like, or smells like.

Rename each of the following products by replacing the word *nice*. Write the new names at the bottom of the page. A sample has been done for you.

Fizzy Soda

Don't Always Say Said

If you overuse a word in a story, you can make your readers dizzy. That's why it's important to watch out for words that are repeated.

Here's your chance to practice. The word *said* is used ten times in the following story. Cross out at least seven of those *saids*. Above the crossed-out word write a new word taken from your head or from the following list: asked, bragged, complained, demanded, laughed, replied, shouted, sputtered, thundered.

The Lazy Worker

"The boss is coming to see if everyone is working," said the clerk.

Suddenly the boss walked into the warehouse.

"I said he was going to come," said the clerk.

"Shhhh," said another worker, trying to look busy.

The boss walked around and studied each person. He stopped in front

of a young man who was not doing anything.

"How much do you get paid a week?" said the boss.

"One hundred dollars," said the man.

"You're fired!" said the boss. "Here's your pay for the week. Now go."

"Thanks," said the young man as he put the hundred dollars in his

pocket. Then off he went.

"Let that be a lesson to you," said the boss to the other workers.

"By the way, what did that man I fired do around here?"

"Nothing," said the foreman. "He's just the delivery man."

Don't Go Wrong With Go

A writer often wants to paint a picture in the reader's mind. Unclear or vague words like *go* or *guy* don't help. When you find them in your writing, try to replace them with more exact words.

1. In each of the sentences below, cross out the word *go*. Above it write a more exact word. Find a word in your head or use one of the following: *climb, dive, fly, gallop, march, sail, shoot, skip, slither, soar, stomp,* and *swing*.

A. Did that three-masted ship go away?

B. I never saw a horse go around the track so fast.

C. We watched the airplane go through the storm.

D. The snakes go through the grass.

E. Who saw the monkey go through the trees?

F. Look at that seal go into the water.

G. Why did the cat go up the tree?

H. Look at that eagle go through the clouds.

I. Watch that elephant go through the high grass.

J. Look at that army go through town.

K. Everyone saw the rocket go into the sky.

2. Write a sentence that uses *go* or *guy* in a vague way. Have a classmate try to replace that word with one that makes a clearer picture.

The Thing Problem

The word *thing* is easy to use when you're writing. The trouble with it is that half the time your readers won't know what you're talking about. To make sure that doesn't happen, try not to use the word too often. Instead, get a clear picture of what you're writing about. Then use its correct name.

1. In the following sentences, replace the word *thing*.

A. I couldn't write because my thing was out of ink.

B. We didn't hear a thing you said.

C. He wanted a thing to cut his nails.

D. Do you have a quarter to put into the parking thing so we won't get a ticket?

E. The thing that turns on the TV is broken.

F. Did you bring the thing so we can play baseball?

G. I left my thing at home so I got wet in the rainstorm.

H. We were sitting so far away I needed a thing to see the game better.

2. Write a sentence that includes the word *thing* and have a friend try to replace *thing* with a clearer word.

One Word Can Be Better Than Two

Sometimes we use two or more words instead of the single, clearer word we should use.

1. Replace the underlined words in the following sentences with a single word. A sample has been done for you.

A. The children ~~walked slowly~~ *strolled* home.

B. He <u>softly said</u> my name.

C. She <u>held</u> the money <u>tightly</u>.

D. The animal <u>made a sad noise</u>.

E. I <u>got</u> out of bed <u>quickly</u>.

F. I <u>pulled strongly</u> on the rope.

G. I <u>closed</u> the door <u>with a loud bang</u>.

H. Who was <u>knocking loudly</u> on the door?

I. "Watch out for the rattlesnake," she <u>said in a loud voice</u>.

J. They <u>quickly drank</u> down their milk.

2. In each of the following sentences, cross out at least two words and replace them with a single word.

K. The mean dog ran quickly after me.

L. The car went quickly along the highway.

M. "Come over here," my friend said in a very soft voice.

Improving Sentences

- breaking apart run-ons
- varying sentence forms
- clarifying pronoun references

Grammar taught in isolation can drive students and teachers crazy. On the other hand, grammar, as it relates to the editing process, is a valued tool. It enables careful writers to check and repair their sentences whether in stories, essays, or poems.

A detailed treatment of grammar is beyond the scope of this book, but the following activities may suggest a start.

EDITING RUN-ON SENTENCES. *Worksheet 23,* Spaghetti Sentences, gives practice in breaking up run-on sentences. To extend the activity, have students prepare run-on worksheets by running together sentences found in the daily newspaper, a textbook, or elsewhere.

CHECKING SUBJECT/VERB AGREEMENT. *Worksheet 24,* Actor and Action, asks students to handle subject/ verb problems.

CHECKING PRONOUN REFERENCES. *Worksheet 25,* Stand-In Words, aims to make students more aware of pronoun reference problems

VARYING SENTENCES. *Worksheet 26,* One Plus One Equals One, introduces the idea of sentence combining.

A more creative activity is to have students write 26-sentence ABC stories or essays. The idea is simple. The first word of the first sentence begins with the letter *A.* The first word of the second sentence begins with the letter *B,* and so on to *Z,* which is the first letter of the first word of the twenty-sixth and last sentence. In order to make everything work out, students will be forced to use all sorts of sentence patterns. Try it yourself and you'll see.

Spaghetti Sentences

When spaghetti noodles run together, the meal may be hard to eat. When sentences run together, the writing may be hard to read. That's why you must take care to show where one sentence ends and another begins.

1. The following examples are run-on sentences. Write each one as two separate sentences using the lines under the example. (Hint: The caret ∧ shows you where a period or question mark is needed. Use a punctuation mark at the end of a sentence.)

A. The most common last name in the U.S. is Smith∧the most popular first name for males is William.

_____

_____

B. How big is your heart∧it's about the same size as your fist.

_____

_____

2. This time you figure out how to break apart each run-on sentence.

C. Americans seem to like peanuts the average American will eat 200 pounds of this food in a lifetime.

_____

_____

D. Have you seen bumps on your tongue they're your taste buds.

_____

_____

Actor and Action

Every sentence needs a subject and a verb. The subject tells who or what the sentence is about. The verb tells what's happening in the sentence. The verb must match the subject. For example, when there's just one car zooming along, the sentence will be:

The car zooms along.

When there are two or more cars, the verb changes:

The cars zoom along.

1. In the following sentences, the subjects and verbs don't match. Fix the sentences by changing the underlined verbs.

A. The grass _are_ always greener on the other side of the fence.

B. A rolling stone _gather_ no moss.

C. Two heads _is_ better than one.

D. Don't bite the hand that _feed_ you.

E. Never _looks_ a gift horse in the mouth.

F. If the shoe fits, _wears_ it.

G. A bird in the hand _are_ worth two in the bush.

2. Write a sentence in which the subject and verb don't match. See if a friend can edit your example.

Stand-In Words

Stand-in actors replace movie stars in some scenes. Pronouns — special words that take the place of nouns — do the same job in writing. In the following example, the pronoun it stands for money.

"Where's the money? Did you spend it?"

There are many different pronouns: she, he, him, her, hers, his, they, them, their, and so on. The trick is picking the right one. It wouldn't make sense to write:

"Where's the money? Did you spend *them*?"

Each of the following examples has a pronoun mistake. Cross out the underlined pronoun and replace it with one that makes sense.

A. The elephant's trunk is as useful as a person's hand. <u>*They*</u> can be used for feeding, digging, holding things, and even untying knots.

B. The Navy has taught whales how to find torpedoes and other objects. <u>*It*</u> can swim down nearly one-third of a mile.

C. If a cockroach touches you, <u>*they*</u> may hurry away and clean itself.

D. Sharks can see ten times clearer than a human being can. That's what makes <u>*him*</u> so dangerous to swimmers.

E. A snail may be the best pet since <u>*they*</u> can go for years without food.

F. Using modern machines, one farmer can care for 20,000 chickens. This includes feeding <u>*it*</u> and collecting <u>*its*</u> eggs.

G. Kangaroo mothers may weigh 60,000 times more than <u>*her*</u> newborn babies.

H. The archer fish captures flies by shooting <u>*it*</u> with drops of water.

One Plus One Equals One

If all your sentences are the same length or start with the same words, your readers may be bored. Watch out for that problem when you read over your work. If you notice that most of your sentences are short, try to put them together to make longer sentences.

Here's your chance to practice that important skill. Rewrite each example below as a single sentence. With some you may need to add such words as *and* or *because*. You may also have to leave words out.

A. I'm hungry. I'll eat.

_____

B. It rained today. It didn't rain yesterday.

_____

C. My cat ran away. Then the mice came out to play.

_____

D. I'm not very brave. Still, I like scary movies.

_____

E. I like football. I like baseball. I don't enjoy fishing.

_____

F. First my shoelace broke. Then my bike had a flat tire.

_____

G. I had no money. Therefore, I could not go to the circus.

_____

Catching Spelling Mistakes

- identifying spelling demons
- correcting spelling errors

Students don't have to be good spellers to catch spelling mistakes in their writing. Most spelling errors involve mixing up simple words such as *its* and *it's* or *went* and *when*.

When it comes to editing for spelling, the key is uncertainty — being able to spot words that *might* be misspelled. Perhaps more important, students need to learn the value of turning out a finished piece of writing that is spelled correctly.

CREATING AWARENESS. The daily edit (see the Introduction) is probably the best way to develop the skills and habits needed to catch spelling mistakes.

GUIDED PRACTICE. As a simple practice, dictate three to five sentences dealing with a subject the class is studying. Choose sentences that contain words that are difficult to spell. When you're finished, go over the spelling of the difficult words with the students and have them correct any misspellings. This practice will help students become aware of the necessity of checking spelling.

EDITING THE REAL WORLD. To increase their mastery, experienced editors mentally correct words outrageously spelled on signs and packages. *Worksheet 27*, Seller Misspellers, lets students practice this art by editing product names that appear in a store window; *Worksheet 28*, License Plates, is about "correcting" vanity plates. In *Worksheet 29*, Silly Headlines, newspaper-style headlines need spelling corrections.

USING EDITING MARKS. *Worksheet 30*, Ridding Riddles of Spelling Mistakes, asks students to deal with a text that has been marked for spelling problems. Finally, *Worksheet 31*, Double-Checking Your Spelling, provides a realistic simulation in the form of a book review containing spelling problems.

Seller Misspellers

1. Find the spelling mistake in the store window. Write the correct spelling in the space below the picture.

2. On another piece of paper, draw a store window that contains other misspelled words. See if a friend can catch and correct the mistakes.

LICENSE PLATES

Look closely at the special license plates below. You'll see that some of them are spelled wrong. Your job is to write the correct spelling in the blank under each plate.

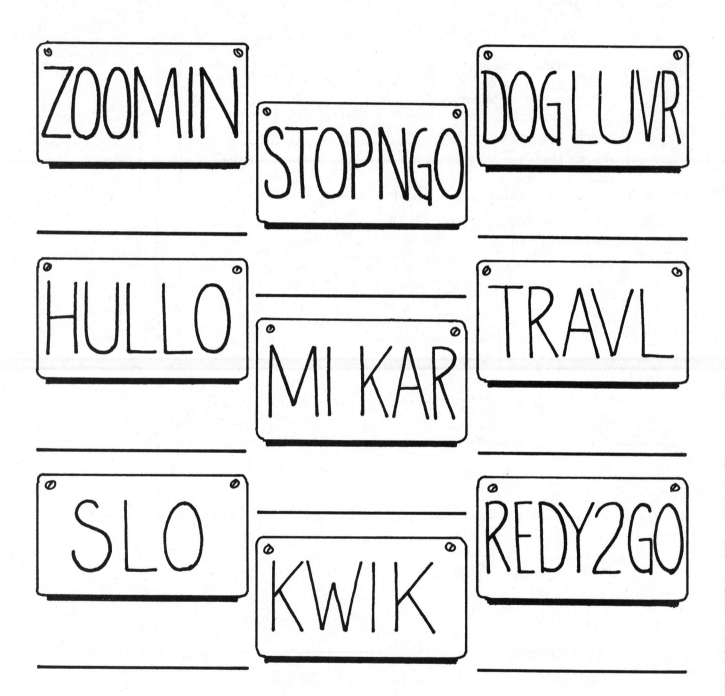

Silly Headlines

1. The following headlines are silly because of one wrong letter in each of them. When you find the mistake, cross out the word and replace it with the correct word.

A. Robber Breaks into Mouse and Steals China

B. Barber Ship on Main Street Has Oldest Barber Pole in Town

C. New Cat Models Offer Better Gas Mileage and Brighter Colors

D. Law Says Owners Must Keep Their Logs on Leashes

E. Dentists Meet to Discuss Toot Decay

F. Socks Move Higher on Wall Street

G. Citizens March Against Higher Taxis

H. Food Waters Drive Many from Their Homes

I. Snow and Ice Store Closes Schools

J. Old Church Bull Rings for Last Time

2. Write two silly headlines that mix up a pair of words. You might use some of the following words or think up your own:

food/foot

pan/pin

fish/fist

sale/salt

boat/coat

Ridding Riddles of Spelling Mistakes

1. Each riddle below has a spelling mistake marked with the letters "sp". Cross out the misspelled word and write the correct spelling above it. You may use a dictionary.

EDITING
FIX-UP
TRUCK

A. How can you know when there's an elephant under you're bed?

Answer: You'll be close to the ceiling.

B. Why is the sky sew high up?

Answer: So the birds won't bump their heads against it.

C. Why did Humpty Dumpty have a grate fall?

Answer: He wanted to make up for a bad summer.

D. What do you call an rabbit with fleas?

Answer: Bugs Bunny.

E. What happens went you throw a green rock into the Red Sea?

Answer: It gets wet.

2. You'll find a spelling mistake in each of the following riddles. Mark the mistake with an "sp" and then correct it as you did above.

F. What can you brake without touching it?

Answer: A promise.

G. What's another name four a sleeping bull?

Answer: A bulldozer.

H. When is a car knot a car?

Answer: When it turns into a driveway.

I. What is the easiest way to make a bannana split?

Answer: You cut it in half.

Double-Checking Your Spelling

Good writers check their spelling more than once. They do this to catch mistakes that they missed the first time. Try it yourself. The following book review was already checked once. See if you can find and fix the spelling problems still in it.

EDITING FIX-UP TRUCK

Some Silly Laws

A.   Do you ever feel that some off the rules at school or home are a bit silly?

B.   I'll bet there not as dumb as some of the real laws in Barbara Seulings'

C.   funy book, *You Can't Eat Peanuts In Church And Other Little Known Laws.*

D.   Here are a few examples:

E.   In Star, Mississippi, its against the law ~~two~~ to make fun of public bildings.

F.   In Boston you need a doctor's written O.K. to take a bath. In Reed City,

G.   Michigan, you can't own a cat an a bird. In Maine you brake the law if

H.   you walk along with you're shoelaces untied.

I.   If these laws make you smile, the hole book should give you the giggles.

J.   It may even make you hapy with the rules in your life.

Checking Punctuation

- using commas, periods, question marks, exclamation points, and quotation marks
- indenting paragraphs
- spacing between words

The key to punctuation mastery, for students who are not deaf, is learning to notice the sounds of language: the change in pitch when a question is asked, the pause between two sentences, the loudness of an emphasized word. Once the link between speech and print is understood, remembering the many rules of punctuation almost becomes child's play.

ORAL READING. Have students read aloud punctuation-rich texts on a regular basis. These might include stories with lots of dialogue, newspaper editorials, magazine advertisements, jokes, and scripts. If possible, invite guest readers such as other teachers, actors from the high school drama club, and so on.

LANGUAGE SCOUTING. Have students collect examples of various kinds of punctuation. Make a bulletin board from items found in magazines, newspapers, novels, billboards, bumperstickers, and so on.

FOCUSING ON END PUNCTUATION. *Worksheet 32*, All's Well That Ends Well, challenges students to pick the right ending marks for a series of bumperstickers.

COMMAS, COMMAS, COMMAS. *Worksheet 33*, Commas, Commas, Commas, shows students how to insert commas into a text.

CATCHING "RUN-ON" WORDS. Everyone knows what a run-on sentence is — but what's a run-on word? It's a meaningless "word" that is madewhen the writer carelessly leaves out the space between two ordinary words. An example — *madewhen* — appears in the previous sentence. *Worksheet 34*, Run-On Words, gives students a chance to wrestle with this problem.

INDENTING PARAGRAPHS. *Worksheet 35*, Giving Readers a Break, introduces the editor's mark for showing where paragraphs begin. To provide more practice, simply copy stories and articles without paragraph breaks. Then have students "match wits" with the professionals by indicating where they think paragraphs belong.

SETTING OFF QUOTATIONS. *Worksheet 36*, Putting Words into People's Mouths, explains the use of quotation marks and urges students to make sure they include both pairs of marks.

All's Well That Ends Well

A period (.) is used to end most sentences. If the sentence is a question, then a question mark (?) will be found at the end. When the writer wants to show excitement, an exclamation point (!) may be used.

EDITING FIX-UP TRUCK

1. Decide which punctuation mark belongs at the end of each of the following bumpersticker sentences. (Hint: It's sometimes hard to choose between a period and an exclamation point. Let your ear help you make up your mind which fits.)

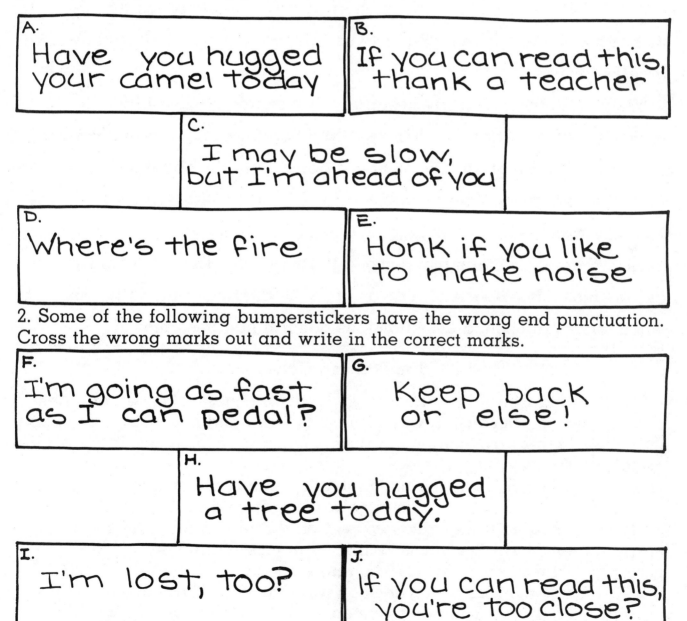

A. Have you hugged your camel today

B. If you can read this, thank a teacher

C. I may be slow, but I'm ahead of you

D. Where's the fire

E. Honk if you like to make noise

2. Some of the following bumperstickers have the wrong end punctuation. Cross the wrong marks out and write in the correct marks.

F. I'm going as fast as I can pedal?

G. Keep back or else!

H. Have you hugged a tree today.

I. I'm lost, too?

J. If you can read this, you're too close?

Commas, Commas, Commas

Your ear can help you figure out where commas belong. Here's a chance to practice.

Fold this sheet at the dotted line. Then listen to the story as it's read aloud. When you hear a short pause in a sentence, use a caret (⌄) to add a comma. The first one has been done for you.

Later, unfold the paper. Use the copy below the line to check your work.

The Panama Canal

The Panama Canal isn't the world's longest⌄widest deepest or oldest canal. However because it was so hard to build and because it is the only man-made waterway that joins two oceans many people call it the world's greatest canal.

In 1881 a French company began to dig a canal across a fifty-mile stretch of land in Panama. In charge was Ferdinand De Lesseps. Earlier De Lesseps had built the famous Suez Canal but this job turned out to be much harder. Mosquitoes caused terrible illness. Within eight years nearly 20,000 workers died. The digging stopped.

In 1907 an American group decided to try the job. The first step was to kill the mosquitoes. When that was done the digging started. By 1914 when the canal opened 10 billion tons of earth had been moved.

- -

The Panama Canal

The Panama Canal isn't the world's longest, widest, deepest, or oldest canal. However, because it was so hard to build and because it is the only man-made waterway that joins two oceans, many people call it the world's greatest canal.

In 1881, a French company began to dig a canal across a fifty-mile stretch of land in Panama. In charge was Ferdinand De Lesseps. Earlier, De Lesseps had built the famous Suez Canal, but this job turned out to be much harder. Mosquitoes caused terrible illness. Within eight years, nearly 20,000 workers died. The digging stopped.

In 1907, an American group decided to try the job. The first step was to kill the mosquitoes. When that was done, the digging started. By 1914, when the canal opened, 10 billion tons of earth had been moved.

Run-On Words

Long ago, words were printed right next to each other like this:

Thewordsrantogether.

Later on, people learned that leaving space makes reading easier. See for yourself:

The words ran together.

That's why you should check your writing to make sure the spaces are where they belong. If you find two words that run together, mark them with this sign: #. It will remind you to leave a space when you rewrite your work.

1. In each of the following fortune cookie fortunes, words run together. Rewrite each fortune with the right spaces.

A. You will leada happy life.

B. What you lost you willfind.

C. Goodluck is yoursforever.

D. You will berichand famous.

2. Put the space mark — # — where it's needed in the following fortunes. Then copy the sentences correctly.

E. Hope forthe best.

F. Thesun willshine on you.

G. Your favorite dreamwill come true.

H. Youwillhavemanyfriends.

Giving Readers a Break

Writers usually break their books into chapters. This makes the books easier to read. The same trick works when you write a short paper. If you break it into parts called *paragraphs*, it will be easier to read.

You can tell where a paragraph begins because the first word is moved a little to the right. This is called *indenting*. In this paragraph the word *You* is indented.

Sometimes writers forget to break a piece of writing into paragraphs. Later, they go back and use this sign —¶— to mark the places where paragraphs should start.

1. On your own paper, rewrite the following joke in four paragraphs. The editing marks tell you where each paragraph should begin.

¶A man was having dinner in a restaurant. When his bowl of soup came, he seemed angry.¶"Is something wrong, sir?" asked the waiter.¶"There certainly is!" said the man. "There's a fly in my soup."¶"Don't worry," smiled the waiter. "The heat will kill that bug in a few seconds."

2. Read the following joke. It should be written in five paragraphs. Your job is to use the paragraph mark —¶— to show where each paragraph should start. Once you've marked the joke, copy it onto another piece of paper.

"Something odd happened last night," said my friend. "What's that?" I asked. "I snored so loud I woke myself up," my friend replied. "What did you do about your problem?" I wanted to know. "Nothing to it," said my friend. "I just got up and went to sleep in the next room."

Putting Words into People's Mouths

The words that characters say in a story is called *dialogue*. It's set off from the other words by quotation marks: " ". These marks come in pairs — they go at the beginning of a speech and at the end.

When a speech has two parts, each part must have its own pair of quotation marks. Here's an example:

"It's time," I said, "to go."

Put in the missing quotation marks from the following joke. Use this editor's mark: ⌄.

The Duck's Bill

One day a hungry duck came into a restaurant and sat down at the counter.

I'll have tuna on white bread," he said, "but no pickles, please.

The owner brought the sandwich.

"Very good, said the duck when he finished. It's just the way I like it.

The owner, thinking the duck wouldn't know much about money, wrote out a bill for fifteen dollars. The duck was shocked but, not liking to argue, paid the money and got up to leave.

You know," said the owner, you're the first duck we've ever had in this restaurant.

I'm not surprised, replied the duck. At the prices you charge, you won't be getting many others, I can promise you.

Preparing the Final Manuscript

- using all the editing skills at once
- preparing final copy

This section gives students practice in dealing with more than one problem in a text and in turning an edited manuscript into a final manuscript.

EDITING CAPTIONS. *Worksheet 37*, Editing Captions, provides students with short pieces of copy to edit and rewrite.

EDITING A LETTER. *Worksheet 38*, Editing a Letter, involves editing a piece of writing. It reminds young writers that editing is important with all types of writing, not just school assignments.

EDITING A STORY. *Worksheet 39*, Editing a Story, provides the most challenging editing exercise in the book. If this one is too much for your students on an individual basis, you might do it as a class editing exercise.

Editing Captions

The following captions have many problems. Read them carefully and you'll find spelling mistakes, fact mistakes, extra words, missing words, and so on. Mark up each caption using the editing marks that you've learned. Then write a new copy of the caption.

A. A mean-looking dog chased to scared-looking cats up tree today

B. Happy Hippo's knew TV talk show is now the program top on the air. Its the show every one is talking about?

C. Two flying saucers are seen zoom by the Empire State Building yesterday they were seen by million of people

Editing a Letter

Letters that you write to your friends need as much careful editing as your school papers.

Here's a chance to practice. Use the editing marks you've learned to correct the many problems in the following letter. You may need to use a dictionary.

When you're done, copy the letter neatly. Be careful not to make any new mistakes.

145 madison Place

New York, New York 10016

March19, 1933

Dear Mom

I want you to no that Ive arrived safe sound in New York City this is an interesting place to be. There are million of people hear, but I haven't found any big apes apes like myself yet. People here do get upset easily? For example, yester day I was out take a walk and I accidentally knocked down a few building. Everyone were yelling and screaming within a few seconds, police drove up in cars with things on top that made loud noises. To get away from all off that, I climbed up a tell skyscraper called "The Empire State Building. It gives you an amazing view of the hole city.

That's it four now.

Love,

Kong

Editing a Story

The following fable needs lots of editing. If you read it carefully, you'll find extra words, missing words, misspelled words, missing punctuation, wrong punctuation, unclear words, run-on words, run-on sentences, and other problems, too.

Your job is to use the editing marks you've learned to improve this story. When you're done, copy the story neatly on another piece of paper.

The Fox and the Crow

The fox was out for walk one day went he saw the crow sitting on a branch off a tree? In the crow's mouth was a piece of yummy-looking cheese the chese made hungry the fox. "I'd sure like a a bite of that cheese," he said. "Would you like to share it with me." The crow shook her head but but kept her beak shut tight on the cheese the fox thought for a while and then said, "I'm not really interested in the cheese," he said. "I came looking for you because I wanted to hear you're wonderful voice. Would you sing for me? The crow wasso pleased to hear these words that he began a song. But no sooner had she opened her mouth than the cheese fell down, right onto the fox's tongue. As he swallowed the treat he said, "Here's some advice in return for the thing. Don't bee fooled by flattery.

PROGRAM

Assessing Skills

The odds must be ten to one that your incoming students will know little or nothing about editing. If you aren't the betting type, however, you may wish to begin your program by finding out just what your class understands about revising first drafts. In this case, choose among the following diagnostic activities. Later in the year you might repeat the assessment to prove to your students — and you — that progress is underway.

ACTIVITIES. Here are suggested diagnostic activities:

1. Have students give their definition or interpretation of "editing." This can be done in writing or orally.

2. Give students a short paragraph to edit for content errors. (You may want to give sophisticated students several paragraphs). Initially, include those skills introduced in previous years. Later, use skills covered during the current year.

3. Give students a short paragraph to edit for errors.

4. Have students identify proofreading symbols. This can be done in a matching format or with flash cards.

Defining Editing

As long as students think of editing as punishment, they are not likely to develop the skills needed to improve their first drafts. The following activities aim to give children a more rational, positive understanding of this creative act.

DISPLAYING EDITING ARTIFACTS. The Resources section of this book includes edited manuscripts by a variety of writers. Collect additional examples by writing — or having students write — to their favorite book authors as well as local word users such as journalists, business people, lawyers, politicals, speech givers, and ad writers. A bulletin board of such materials should help convince students that editing is a natural part of writing and a sign of maturity and intelligence.

POSTING A DEFINITION OF EDITING. Feel free to adapt the following:

> Editing is the step in writing when the author becomes his or her own first reader. This step gives the person a chance to make changes that make the writing clear and more interesting. Editing also includes letting other people read the words and tell how they think the writing might be improved.

LINKING EDITING TO SIMILAR FAMILIAR ACTIVITIES. Figures of speech can help students learn that editing is a universal step in the creative process. Here's a simile you might discuss with your class:

> Imagine you're getting dressed. After you put your clothes on, you use a mirror to check how you look. In a way you stand outside yourself. If you spot a problem such as a rip in your shirt, you fix it or you change your shirt. Later, if a friend notices that a button is missing and tells you about it, you say "Thanks" because what your friend told you can help you improve your appearance.

> In the same way, after you write a rough draft, you must become your own first reader. If you spot a problem such as an extra word or a missing period, you fix it. Later, your teacher or a classmate may read your paper and give you hints for making it better. Again, you should say "Thanks" because the suggestions can help you do a better job

GIVING STUDENTS STEP-BY-STEP EDITING DIRECTIONS. The recipe shown on *Worksheets 40A* and *40B* can be simplified for younger students. You might duplicate it as a "take-home teacher" for your students or give a copy to parents.

Editing Recipe Part 1

When writing a first draft, leave room for changes. Skip every other line and use wide margins. 1

Put the draft aside for a while. 2

Before you edit, get a dictionary, pencil, and other needed materials. 3

Decide what problems you'll be looking for— ideas, words, spelling, or everything. 4

Reading your work slowly and aloud may help you spot problems. 5

Editing Recipe Part 2

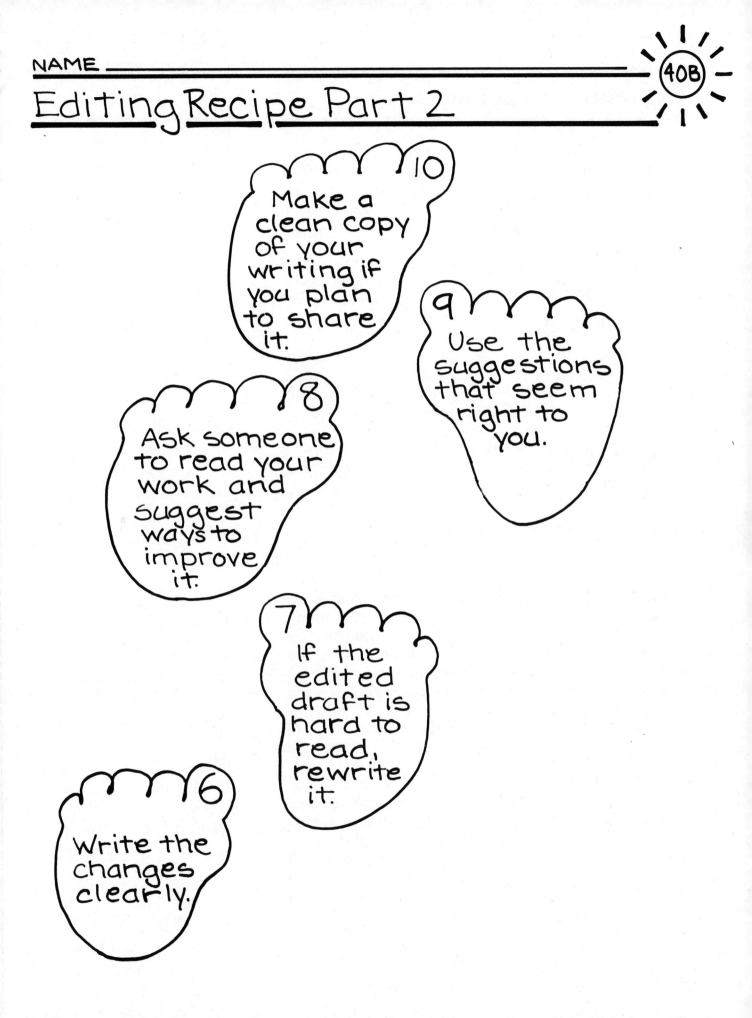

10 Make a clean copy of your writing if you plan to share it.

9 Use the suggestions that seem right to you.

8 Ask someone to read your work and suggest ways to improve it.

7 If the edited draft is hard to read, rewrite it.

6 Write the changes clearly.

Demonstrating Editing

Would-be pilots learn to fly by watching experienced pilots. Likewise, cooks learn from cooks, surgeons from surgeons, and teachers from teachers. Watching an "old pro" not only makes a task clear, it makes it seem possible. No other educational experience provides so much motivation.

If editing seems like a scary, or unmanageable task to students, the reason probably is that they haven't seen anyone do it. The solution is to offer your students many opportunities to watch editors at work marking up rough drafts. Who will do the demonstrating?

THE TEACHER. Whenever you're at the chalkboard, you have a chance to model editing. If you're unsure of a word, write *sp* next to it. If your students are old enough, ask one of them to look up the word. Otherwise, do it yourself.

You can also demonstrate editing when you're directing the class in the daily edit or going over one of the worksheets from this book.

A third possibility is for you to explain the process when you are working with students during a one-on-one conference. (This is the way most professional journalists learned how to edit.)

THE STUDENTS. When students take over the job of correcting the daily edit, they serve as models for each other. They can do the same thing whenever they volunteer to do writing assignments on the board. As they review their work and make corrections, they show the rest of the class what editing is all about.

GUEST WRITERS. In almost every community you can find practicing writers — novelists, poets, journalists, ad writers, letter-to-the-editor writers. Some of these folks will be happy to bring in first drafts and demonstrate editing on the overhead projector.

MEDIA PRESENTATIONS. Many writers share their editing techniques in books, filmstrips, and movies. These packaged demonstrations can prove powerful. Without a doubt the best of such "canned" material is Charles Schultz's *Peanuts* comic strips. Time and again Schultz has his characters model all the basic editing skills in terms even young children can appreciate.

Creating An Editing Environment

Experienced editors can do their work almost anywhere — at a desk, on a plane, in the library, over lunch (but not while watching TV!). On the other hand, novice editors like your students will do better if they edit within a carefully designed environment.

One way to set the stage for the editing act is to establish a classroom editing center. Typically this space will contain a table with several chairs, posters about writing and editing, a bookshelf, and other such furniture.

The editing center should house all the "tools" your editors will need (and that you can afford):

- dictionaries
- thesauruses
- grammar and usage books
- style manuals
- almanacs and other reference books
- scissors, tape, and stapler (for cutting and pasting)
- white-out correction fluid (non-toxic variety)
- colored pencils
- easy-to-remove stick-on flags or labels (3M's "Post-It" brand is a good example) for making editorial comments

Two small "tools" can help students take big strides when it comes time for self-editing. These aids are inexpensive, easy to make, and can be housed in your editing center.

REVISION FOLDERS. Revision folders are actually file folders with a library pocket attached to the front. The pocket is designed to hold specific editing messages from the teacher to the writer: "Check your spelling" or "Add details to the descriptions of your characters." Write this advice on cardboard strips or tongue depressors.

When a student has completed a first draft and is ready for some feedback, have him or her put the manuscript inside a folder. Once you've read the work, you can choose relevant editing-skill strips and slip them into the waiting pocket. The student should consult the strips during the editing process. When this phase of the work is done, the writer may sign up for an editing conference to discuss the changes. (See Conferring with the Teacher, later in this section.)

FLAG PENCILS. Real-life editors use colored pencils to make changes with; so can your student editors. Make Flag Pencils with different-colored pencils indicating various skills. For example, you might put the flag "Capital letters" on a red pencil and "Details" on a green one. You can attach the flags with tape or cement. Laminating the tags and backing them with tagboard will increase durability.

Two "big ticket" items (perhaps already in your school) would be helpful, too:

TAPE RECORDERS. Here's how these often under-utilized machines fit into an editing program. When students complete initial drafts, occasionally have them record their words. While listening to the tape, students should write down changes they feel should be made. Often, a second listening will provide even more editing insights.

WORD PROCESSORS. More and more writers — journalists, novelists, even poets — are using word processors. Why? These machines make editing infinitely simpler. We could give you many arguments proving the case but none is so powerful as trying the equipment yourself.

Word processors, however, do not make obsolete the other items described above, not even the colored pencils. A number of professionals who write and edit "electronically" still do some or even most of the revising on paper.

Developing Student Style Manuals

Writers in the "real world" often depend on the guidelines of a style manual to help them prepare their manuscripts. Student writers can also benefit from this type of handy reference, especially if they create their own style manuals that include the information and special symbols needed for the writing and editing process.

As students create their manuals, you can use the following suggestions to help them on their way:

1. Give your students clear reasons for taking the time to create style manuals. Let them know that the activity is not just "busy work" but will actually help them during writing and editing. Show students several standard style manuals that are often used by adult writers.

2. Compose a style manual yourself that the students can use as a model.

3. Let students compose their manuals over a period of time. In this way, each idea they include will be important.

4. Use the time students spend on creating their manuals to review and reinforce writing skills and processes.

5. Have high expectations for the quality of the handwriting and illustrations. Encourage the class to produce booklets they'll be proud of.

WHAT TO INCLUDE. The information students put into their style manuals will depend on their writing experience and specific needs. The following can be considered basic pages to include.

● Cover — Students may design individual style manual covers.

● The writing process — A list and brief explanation of the five steps in the writing process will help young authors write more effectively. (See The Writing Process bulletin board.)

● The editing skills — Setting the editing skills down on paper will help students remember them. (See Resources.)

● The editing symbols — A handy list of the editing symbols will help students revise their work.

● Punctuation — This page should contain a list of the punctuation rules and style customs students should follow.

● Spelling words — Your students may benefit from having a short, easy-to-use list of spelling demons.

Editing All Together (E.A.T.)

The Editing All Together activity is an editing demonstration *with* audience participation. The basic idea is that students help the teacher edit a mock manuscript and then apply the same techniques to their own papers.

To begin Editing All Together, first choose the problems you want to focus on, for example, weak leads and run-on sentences. Next, select a format such as the short story or the friendly letter and create a mock draft. Be sure to double space the manuscript, leave wide margins, and number the lines on the left.

The day before you hold the activity, ask your students to compose a short piece of writing in the same format as your example. They don't need a polished text, just a draft they will edit.

When you begin E.A.T., present your example using the overhead projector or a large piece of paper. While the students read the text, draw a simple evaluation chart like the one shown here. Label the left section "Quality" and the right section "Changes."

When the students have read the paper, ask, "What are some of the quality elements of this writing?" or "What looks correct to you about this paper?" By looking for the positive elements, you'll be off to a strong start.

As the students offer their positive comments, ask the class as a whole to agree or disagree with them. Write all accepted comments in the "Quality" section of the chart.

QUALITY (strengths)	CHANGES
① Descriptions use all senses.	① The ending is a little confusing.
② Each character's voice sounds different.	② The word happy might be used too often.
③ All sentences are correctly punctuated.	③ There are several spelling mistakes.

Now ask the students, "What, if any, suggestions for changes in the content would you make?" Comments should be specific and should refer to a given line. For example:

> "*Once upon a time* in line 1 is a weak beginning for such an exciting story. I'd change the opening to 'ZAP! He appeared in a yellow cloud!' "

Note all suggestions in the margin or text of the dummy using standard editing symbols. At this point, ask for suggestions to improve the mechanics of the mock paper, and include those, too, in the margin or in the text. When there are no further comments, review all the changes with the class and list them on the "Changes" section of the chart.

Now have each student choose one content change (say, wording) and one mechanics change (say, spelling) to zero in on when editing his or her own paper. Have the students write their editing "choices" at the tops of their papers, then begin editing.

E.A.T. clearly is not a one-time activity. In fact, you might go through the exercise twice a week at the start of the school year. The goal would be to teach students the routine of editing. Then, later in the year, you might dust off the activity whenever a new skill is being taught. You can have the whole class E.A.T. together or do the process in small groups.

The big point to remember is that developing editing skills takes lots of time and lots of thoughtful practice.

Solo Editing

Here's the moment of truth. Can we motivate students to edit *on their own*? The following four suggestions are meant to bring about the answer we all want to hear, a great big "YES!"

1. **GIVE AN ASSIGNMENT THAT HAS AN AUTHENTIC PURPOSE.** Few people edit their shopping lists. After all, it doesn't matter how *banana* is spelled as long as you can peel it once you get it home. But when you're writing a complaint letter about a car that turned out to be a lemon, then you'll double-check your spelling.

The point is: To get students to polish what they write, arrange publication opportunities that make a real difference in the lives of the readers. Examples include:

- posters to be displayed in school or around town
- letters to the editor of the local paper
- play scripts that younger students will perform, which therefore must be clear and legible
- crossword puzzles for peers or parents to solve
- children's picture-books that will be catalogued and stored, possibly for many years, in the school library

2. **ALLOT EDITING TIME.** Don't assume students will find time to rework their first drafts. If you budget fifteen minutes for composing a first draft in class, set aside at least ten minutes the following day for editing the manuscript. The *action* of giving precious class time to this work will proclaim louder than words the importance of revision in the creative process.

3. **LIMIT THE EDITING TASK.** Long pieces are tougher to edit than short ones. In general, if you want quality editing, keep the manuscript to a page or less. A thorough reading and reworking of a three-paragraph essay is far better than a sloppy, half-hearted skimming — and then "inking" — of a lengthy "tract."

But what if students, for one reason or another, produce a long first draft? One possibility is to have the students work on the text part by part. Another is to limit a given editing session to a particular problem, for example, word choice.

4. **MAKE SURE STUDENTS KNOW THAT THEY ARE NOT TOTALLY ALONE.** When pilots solo, they can count on ground support. In the same way, most experienced writers welcome the help of "outside" editors to improve their manuscripts. Students need the option, too. The following sections explain how this can be arranged without overburdening the teacher.

Conferring With the Teacher

Most experienced writers like — and need — to confer with an "outside" editor once a readable draft has been completed. This *trial reader* usually offers one or more of the following services: listening to the writer read from his or her work, asking questions, pointing out problems, discussing or debating ideas, giving suggestions, and making corrections.

The editing conference can be just as valuable in the classroom. However, finding the time to prepare, plan, and carry out this activity is no small task. The suggestions below may help.

1. Establish a specific area in the classroom for editing conferences. If the classroom already has an editing center, just adapt the physical setup to encourage face-to-face discussion.

2. Make an "Editor" button to wear when editing students' initial drafts. Showing students during a conference that your role is Editor/Helper, not Critic/Judge, can help to keep students from becoming defensive.

3. Create an Editor's Folder for each assigned writing format. The folder should contain the questions that an editor might ask about that kind of writing. When a student believes an initial draft is complete, she or he uses the Editor's Folder questions as a self-edit to prepare for the editing conference. You can also use the questions to begin the editing conference so the students will know at least some of the questions that will be asked and perhaps feel more at ease.

To make each Editor's Folder, use a standard file folder as the cover. Put the title of the format on the front

INSIDE

Content Revision	Mechanics Revision
• who is the audience for your story?	• Are all words spelled correctly?
• How is your story organized?	• Are all sentences complete thoughts?
• Did you choose a topic that is interesting to you?	• Have you capitalized the first word of each sentence?
• Did you follow your plans?	• _____
• Does your title "grab" your reader's attention?	• _____
• _____	• _____
• _____	

of the folder and let students decorate the folders if you like. On the inside front cover write content questions for the students to answer. On the inside back cover write questions about mechanics.

4. Use an Editing Conference Sign-Up Board to keep track of students who have answered the questions in the Editing Folder and are ready for an editing conference with you. Next to the Sign-Up Board post several activity suggestions for students to work on while waiting for their conferences.

5. Use *Worksheet 41*, Conference Record, to give students a written copy of recommendations and comments made during each editing conference. Students should keep each record sheet with the appropriate initial draft to refer to as revisions are made. At subsequent editing conferences on the same piece of writing, use the same record sheet for comments.

Conference Record Sheet

Name_____

Title of Work_____

_____

First Editing Conference   Date_____

Strengths   Suggestions

_____

Second Editing Conference Date_____

Strengths   Suggestions

_____

Final Comments

_____

Editing Services

PEER EDITING. There won't always be a teacher available to consult with, but one can usually find a friend or colleague near by. That's why it makes sense to show students how to get the most from peer editing.

This kind of collaboration has multiple benefits. The writer gets help in improving his or her work. The peer editor has a chance to sharpen editing skills. Both students get an action lesson in independent learning. And the teacher's paper-reading burden is lightened at least a little.

Students, alas, are not born knowing how to conduct a peer-editing session. Probably the best way to teach them is for you to role-play with a student or a colleague in front of the class. For the manuscript, use a mock draft or an anonymous paper from another year. Pass out copies so the class can follow along.

After the demonstration, have your students practice the skill, also using fake papers. To avoid the popularity contest approach to selecting editing partners, draw lots to pair kids up.

Once students show you that they can be perceptive peer editors, you're set to try the activity for real. The first step is to have everyone independently edit a piece of writing according to the directions on *Worksheet 42 or 43,* Editing Partners record sheets. After completing the first three items on the handout, students should meet with their partners to continue the process. The last two items on the record sheet are to be completed independently. The page is then attached to the edited draft. The teacher may simply check the peer-editor's work or make additional editorial suggestions.

SPECIALIST EDITING SERVICE. The following peer-editing spinoff activity requires students who have mastered a given editing skill. These editing specialists volunteer — or are volunteered — for the job of helping their classmates with punctuation, wording, grammatical, or other particular problems.

While the students are editing, have them wear one of the duplicatable buttons on *Worksheet 44.* Also display their names in the editing center and the times they will be there.

When a student has an initial draft ready for editing, have him or her fill out an Editing Request form *(Worksheet 44)* and attach it to the draft. Then have the student place the draft in the designated section of the editing area to await the suggestions of the Specialist Editor. As the editor checks through the draft, he or she can make brief notes in the paper's margin and longer suggestions on the Specialist Editor Suggestions form *(Worksheet 45)*. The form should be attached to the draft when it is returned to the author.

CROSS-AGE EDITORS. Older students can benefit greatly by serving as editors for younger authors. By providing editing service they can improve their self-concept as well as their questioning, comprehension, observation, and interpersonal skills. Usually, primary-grade teachers are delighted to have student editors' assistance. This useful process, however, needs to be structured and developed very carefully in order for it to be effective for all concerned.

The ideas that follow can help you establish and guide a Cross-Age Editing Service:

STEP 1. The student editor contacts the teacher (at an acceptable time) and is given the name of his or her student author, teacher approval (signature), the date and time the edit will take place, and the type of writing that will be edited. The teacher may elect to speak to all the student editors at once or one by one. When editors have the information they need, they write that information on the Editing Service worksheet (with teacher guidance if needed).

STEP 2. Back in their classroom, student editors role play:
- ways to successfully begin an editing conference
- effective techniques for initial questioning, probing, handling responses, etc.
- appropriate editing comments
- proper marking of papers

STEP 3. Student editors edit the younger authors' papers.

STEP 4. The conference is held. If possible, the consulting teacher should observe in a non-judgmental manner. The student editor should use his or her notes and make constructive editorial comments. When the conference is completed, the student editor writes final comments for the teacher on the worksheet.

STEP 5. The student editor gives the worksheet to the student author's teacher for reading.

STEP 6. The author's teacher, if he or she was able to be at the conference, writes comments on the worksheet.

STEP 7. The completed worksheet is returned to the student editor.

Editing Partners Record: Fiction

Title of Story _____

Author _____ Editing partner _____

(Check each item when it's completed.)

On your own (before the conference):

☐ Read your story to yourself.

☐ Check the beginning and the ending.

☐ Check the order of events.

☐ Cut parts that aren't needed.

☐ Add parts that are needed.

☐ Make sure you can "see" the characters.

☐ Listen to the dialogue.

With your partner:

☐ Read your story aloud with expression.

Ask your partner the following questions and listen carefully to the answers. (You may wish to take notes.)
☐ Is the beginning interesting? Any suggestions?
☐ Are the characters believable? Any suggestions?
☐ Are the problems and solutions clear? Any suggestions?
☐ Does the dialogue sound real? Any suggestions?
☐ Is the ending satisfying? Any suggestions?
☐ Are there any other comments or suggestions?

On your own (after the conference):

☐ Make changes based on your partner's suggestions.

Check
☐ spelling
☐ punctuation

When finished, attach this sheet to your first draft.

Editing Partners Record: Nonfiction

Title of work _____

Kind of writing (book report, speech, etc.) _____

Author _____ Editing partner _____

(Check each item when it's completed.)

On your own (before the conference):

☐ Read your work to yourself.

☐ Cut details that aren't needed.

☐ Add details that are needed.

☐ Check the lead (beginning) and conclusion (ending).

☐ Check the order of ideas. Rearrange if necessary.

☐ Double-check the facts.

☐ Check the title. Make sure it fits the paper.

With your partner:

☐ Read your work aloud in a clear voice.

Ask your partner the following questions and listen carefully to the answers. (You may wish to take notes.)
☐ Is the beginning interesting? Any suggestions?
☐ Are the facts interesting? Any suggestions?
☐ Should anything be cut or added?
☐ Does the order make sense? Any suggestions?
☐ Does the ending make sense? Any suggestions?
☐ Does the title fit? Any suggestions?
☐ Are there any other comments or suggestions?

On your own (after the conference):

☐ Make changes based on your partner's suggestions.

Check
☐ spelling
☐ punctuation

When finished, attach this sheet to your first draft.

Specialist Editing Services

EDITOR

NAME

SKILL

EDITOR

NAME

SKILL

EDITING REQUEST

_____ would like
AUTHOR

editing suggestions on

☆ _____

☆ _____

☆ _____

Date of request _____

Editing Suggestions

SUGGESTIONS

Editor _____

Title of work _____

Author of work _____

Date _____

Suggestions: _____

_____

_____

_____

_____

_____

_____

_____

_____

_____

Editing Service

EDITING SERVICE

1 Author's name_____
Author's teacher_____ Author's room___

2 Editor's name_____
Editor's teacher_____ Editor's room___

3 Date & time of editing conference_____

4 Type of writing (story, letter, etc)_____

5 Title of writing_____

6 Content questions to be covered: ideas, clarity, etc. (specified by author's teacher)
_____
_____

7 Mechanics questions to be covered: spelling, punctuation, etc. (specified by author's teacher)
_____
_____

8 Editor's notes about manuscript:
_____
_____□ more on back

9 Teacher's comments to the editor:_____
_____
_____
_____
_____

(Please return this sheet to the editor.)

Involving Parents in Editing

Parents can give your editing program a big lift if you explain what you're doing and tell parents how they can help.

Once you've got your writing program underway, plan a parent's orientation session. During that program explain the step-by-step writing process and the key role editing plays in it. Be specific about how you teach writing and editing skills. Then show how they're practiced in both mock and real writing assignments. Outline the system of communication you will be using for homework assignments and discuss your approach to giving feedback and grades.

Since action speaks louder than words, invite parents to try a daily edit exercise or one of the worksheets from this book. Another possibility is to stage a student editing demonstration. You can end the program by listing the ways parents can help their children during the editing step: by listening, reacting, and offering suggestions. Let parents know that taking over and actually making changes is *not* helpful.

HOME-SCHOOL COMMUNICATION. To supplement your presentation and to reach parents who could not attend, you may wish to send home a letter explaining the writing process and the importance of revision and practice in developing writing skills. *Worksheet 47*, Parent Letter, is a sample letter from a fifth/sixth grade classroom that was sent home attached to two edited draft examples.

Whenever an initial draft is to be worked on at home, it is helpful to attach a brief note to it outlining expectations. A form such as *Worksheet 48*, A Note to Parents, can be filled in by students with your assistance and then stapled to the home-bound drafts. Stamping "Draft" on a manuscript will also remind parents that the paper is a work in progress and not to be considered a finished product.

Parent Letter

September

Dear Parents of Student Authors,

Our class is already well into our third writing assignment. Writing is a part of our everyday activities.

This year these steps will be taken for each writing assignment:

1. Understand the topic and format (teacher and students working together)
2. Develop ideas (brainstorm and research)
3. Write an initial draft (getting ideas down quickly and leaving space for revisions)
4. Edit (Two steps: revising content and then mechanics)
5. Publish (final copy)

These are the steps authors in the "real world" use, too!

Step 4 — Edit — is most important. During this step students clarify ideas and rework words until all are acceptable. If your son or daughter brings home an initial draft for editing, you can help in the following ways:

● Ask that the draft be read aloud. Encourage any needed self-editing by the student.
● Sit with your child, read the draft, and ask questions about the piece's content.
● Point out needed mechanics revisions by making a mark at the end of the line including the error. Let your child find the specific error and make the actual change.

Student authors usually want to share their work. However, they can become defensive unless adults encourage them. Be positive, be clear, be an editor/helper, not a harsh critic.

Learning to write well is a most important life skill. Thanks for helping your student author on the path to developing skill and competence.

If you have any questions, please contact me.

Sincerely,

P.S. Be sure to ask to read your child's writing! Your interest means a great deal.

Note to Parents

Writing Takes Work

This assignment is _____

_____

_____

completed by: The initial draft should be
_____

Please assist with:

_____

_____

_____

_____

_____

Writing Takes Work

This assignment is _____

_____

_____

completed by: The initial draft should be
_____

Please assist with:

_____

_____

_____

_____

_____

Giving Feedback/Grades

When basketball players shoot, they need to know what happens to the ball. Does it swish through the hoop, hit the rim, or bounce off the backboard? Without knowing the answer — receiving feedback — players can't know what adjustments, if any, to make.

Feedback is essential for success in virtually every human endeavor, from pounding in a nail to painting a picture to making soup. Certainly it's vital in writing.

Writers get feedback in two ways. First, they can observe their reader's immediate responses — laughter, tears, gasps, giggles, withdrawal, rebuttals, yawns, or specific actions such as following directions. To generate such feedback, have students regularly share their work throughout the school and in the community at large.

The second kind of feedback involves having an "outside" editor. This person, who can be a friend, a boss, a teacher, or a professional, helps the writer by giving specific verbal comments orally or in writing. These comments take such forms as:

- Reactions — "I laughed at the point in your story when..."
- Questions — "Why did the dog start barking here?" (These should be authentic questions, not disguised commands — "Wouldn't you like to add an example here?")
- Observations — "You used the word *maybe* at least ten times on this page."
- Suggestions — "You might try to write a snappier ending."
- Error notations — These can be explicit — for example, writing "sp" next to a misspelled word — or general — putting a check or a question mark next to a problem, thus requiring the writer to figure out what needs to be done. For young or inexperienced writers, most error notations should be explicit.
- Corrections — These are actual changes made in the text. Generally, the outside editor should *not* make corrections since that tends to reduce the writer's initiative and involvement.

There are two exceptions. First, it's sensible to make a correction when you're teaching a skill that the student hasn't yet learned. The marks on the paper then become an "object lesson."

Second, when the teacher, in the role of "publisher," prepares a manuscript for publication outside the classroom, corrections are in order. "Outside the classroom" includes everything from a bulletin board display in the main hallway to a letter sent to the legislature.

If a student objects to having the teacher edit work before presenting it to strangers, the editing should not be made. However, the teacher also is under no obligation to assist in the publication of such material. After all, when unfinished error-filled student writing appears in public, it isn't the child who gets the blame. Nor is it the parents. Who is it? You guessed it.

Two kinds of feedback are *not* helpful. The first is *vague praise*, such as "Good work" or "Terrific." Since comments like these don't tell the writer exactly what is good, he or she isn't sure how to build on the success.

The second kind of unproductive feedback is *vague criticism*, such as "Poor work" or "Not up to your usual level." Without specifying the problem, criticism merely makes the writer feel bad.

What about grades? They need to be discussed in any book that deals with writing, but don't expect the definitive answer here. There isn't one.

Grades, whether in the form of a letter (A, B, C, D, or..ugh, F), a number (87%), or a picture symbol such as a smiley face, offer little useful information. Generally they tell students their relative position in class, something most kids already know. Grades do *not* show anyone *how* to do a better job. Their main function seems to be to help colleges pick students.

Still, grades are a fact of life. To lessen their negative impact, we recommend the following strategies:

1. Never grade a first draft.
2. Never grade practice papers.
3. Don't grade every assignment. Otherwise, students will think the purpose of writing is to obtain a grade rather than to communicate.
4. Do what you can to get students to pay less attention to the grades you give and more attention to their readers' and editors' comments.

Some teachers never put grades on writing, only comments. The grades go into the grade book. Students must first read the comments and then are given the grade orally. This may not be the ultimate solution but we'll give those folks an A for trying.

BULLETIN
BOARDS

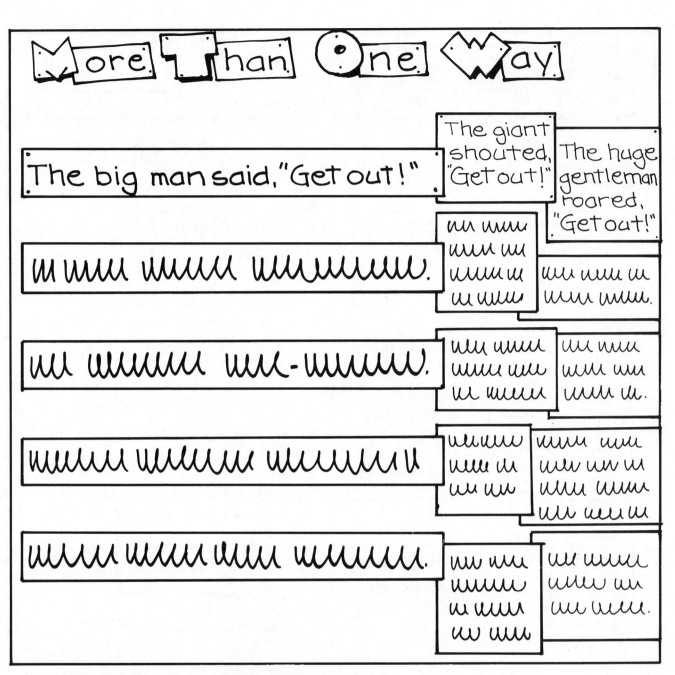

This board is designed to help students understand that there is often more than one way to edit a draft.

To make the bulletin board, post a number of sentences that contain problems. Challenge the students, working independently or in pairs, to improve each sentence in as many different ways as possible. Sometimes there will be only one way to edit a sentence correctly. Sometimes there will be many ways. When the students have finished editing, post their results next to the original draft sentences. Then discuss each alternative.

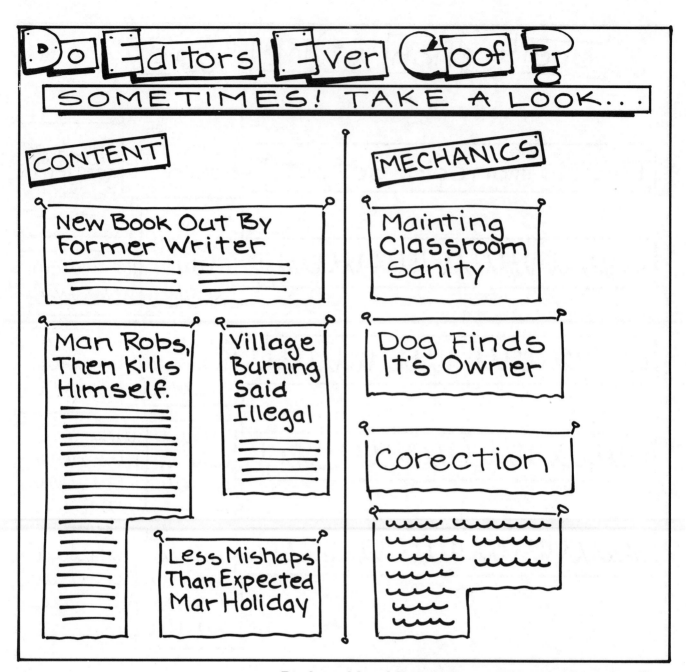

Do Editors Ever Goof?

SOMETIMES! TAKE A LOOK...

CONTENT

New Book Out By
Former Writer

Man Robs,
Then Kills
Himself.

Village
Burning
Said
Illegal

Less Mishaps
Than Expected
Mar Holiday

MECHANICS

Mainting
Classroom
Sanity

Dog Finds
It's Owner

Corection

Real-world publications are filled with errors. Turn your students into "error scouts" at the beginning of your editing program by challenging them to bring in examples of errors from newspapers and other publications.

As items are brought into the classroom, post them on the bulletin board under the proper heading — content or mechanics errors. Then, after several weeks of collecting, hold a class discussion that includes the following questions:

Which type of publication has the sloppiest editing?

Which type of error occurs most often?

THE WRITING PROCESS

1 Choose a topic.

2 Develop the idea.

3 Write a first draft.

4 Edit the draft.

5 Publish.

This bulletin board's focus is the entire writing process. It will give students an overall structure for each writing assignment and let them know when editing or revising will take place.

Using a short objective format such as a paragraph description of an object, guide the students through the entire writing process. After you work through the piece, have the students reflect on the activity in a class discussion. What happened during each of the writing steps? Then, using index cards or pieces of construction paper, have students write short comments about each step. Post these remarks for students to read.

"Why should I edit?" your students will probably ask. Since they usually see only published writing, they assume that words, once written, are in final form and ready to be published. This bulletin board shows how successful real-world authors write, edit, and edit some more. It will let your students know that "authors always edit" to improve their work.

To make the bulletin board, tack up copies of edited drafts of successful authors (see Resources). Also encourage students to write to their favorite novelist, reporter, cartoonist, or other author for additional samples to put on the board.

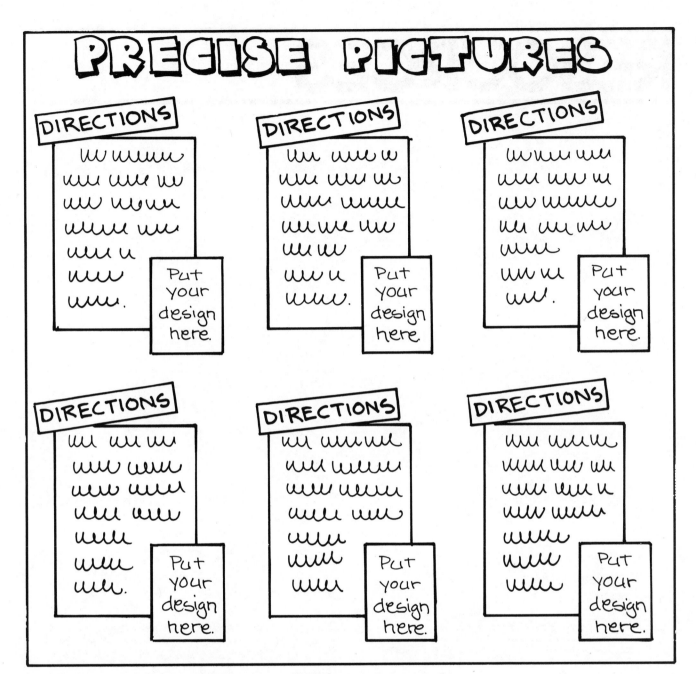

The Precise Pictures bulletin board is the result of an accurate writing and editing activity. Students begin by individually composing an abstract design and writing directions for drawing that figure. Then two students exchange the written directions for their design and try to sketch each other's picture. If the new drawing does not match the original, the writer should edit his or her directions.

Next, have students post their directions on the bulletin board. Classmates will then read the words and try to draw the designs. The results, placed in envelopes on the board, will give the writers clear feedback on how well they edited their directions.

RESOURCES

Edited Draft from a Speech by Harry S. Truman

letter to President Monroe, urging the adoption of what we now know as

the Monroe Doctrine, he wrote:

"Nor is the occasion to be slighted which this proposition

offers of declaring our protest against the atrocious violations of the

rights of nations by the interference of any one in the internal affairs

of another."

We, like Jefferson, have witnessed atrocious violations *of the rights*

of nations.

We, too, have regarded them as occasions not to be slighted.

We, too, have declared our protest.

We must ~~implement~~ that protest *by making* *effective* aid ~~to~~ those peoples whose

freedoms are endangered by foreign pressures.

We must take a positive stand. It is no longer enough to *merely* *say*

~~possible that~~ "we don't want war." *We must* ~~It is to~~ act, in time - ahead of time -

~~And~~ to stamp out the smouldering beginnings of any conflict that may threaten

to spread over the world.

We know how the fire starts. We have seen it before ~~. . .~~

aggression by the strong against the weak, openly by the use of armed

forces *and* ~~or~~ secretly by infiltration. We know how the fire spreads. And

we know how it ends.

Edited Draft from *Good For Me* by Marilyn Burns

chains have been started since the White Castle. Mc
Donalds is the biggest, with over ~~2000~~ 4000 stands in the United
States and in foreign countries, too. Hamburgers in all
of these McDonalds stands are prepared to the same standards.
Each is .221 inches thick, 3.875 inches in diameter,
weighs 1.6 ounces, takes 55 seconds to put together, and
~~fi ti~~ if it isn't sold in 10 minutes, it's thrown away. The
Tartars could never have imagined that their mounds of
meat would become precision affairs. ~~And in 1973, McDonalds' sales were a billion and a half dollars. That's
a lot of hamburgers.~~

Do you know what's the biggest number of hamburgers
anyone ever ate at one sitting? Give that a thought. ~~The~~ In 1976,
someone ate 17 hamburgers in 30 minutes. ~~record was set in 1955 when a man ate 77.~~ Quite a mouthful.

What's your hamburger quota? How many do you eat?
Do you know? Keep a tally for a week and see. Who do you
know eats the most hamburgers? Organize your friends and
ask them all to keep their statistics and see how you
shape up.

Could you live on hamburgers? Nope. As a food, they are OK to eat, ~~They are Not that they're not OK food to eat~~, but they're not a well-balanced diet.
Most of the hamburger chains sell only hamburgers, french-
fries, shakes, and desserts. No other vegetables, besides
potatoes, and No fruits are available. That's Not good if you're eating your
meals there as a steady diet.

Draft manuscript from *Good For Me* by Marilyn Burns. Reprinted with permission of the author.

Edited Draft from *The Mysterious Zetabet* by Scott Corbett

Zig Zag Zack

-1-

Zachary Zwicker was hungry and bored, but his mother ~~was~~ told him he could not have anything to eat until he ~~had~~ finished his homework.

He sat ~~under a tree~~ in his back yard wishing he were somewhere else---any place where there was plenty of food and no homework to do.

~~He~~ Zack looked at ~~the~~ a list of words ~~in his workbook.~~ He was supposed to write ~~them~~ down in alphabetical order. ~~But~~ The alphabet bored him. The only thing he liked about it was the last letter. He liked words that began with "Z". With a name like his, this was not surprising.

~~Just looking at that list of words made him feel sleepy.~~ So instead of doing his homework, he leaned back against ~~the~~ a tree, closed his eyes, and thought about his name and his initials. Z. Z. What wonderful initials for anyone to have. Z.Z. . . . Z-z-z-z-z . . .

Suddenly Zack was whisked away into space. When he opened his eyes he was in a cage being carried along a crooked road by four hooded figures. The road twisted back and forth so sharply he was jolted from side to side against the bars.

Before he had time to do more than feel scared, a tall man in a flashy uniform came galloping up. He was mounted on an odd-looking animal.

Edited Draft/Final Version of a Hallmark Card

This dragon's not wicked
~~like~~ as most dragons are~~--~~
~~It's~~ He's the ~~nicest~~ kindest,
most~~-~~well-behaved ~~monster~~ dragon by far~~.~~,
And today ~~it~~ he is bringing
this big wish ~~just~~ for you
As only a really ~~swell~~ nice dragon
can do.

FOR YOU, GRANDSON

This dragon's not wicked
as most dragons are--
He's the kindest,
most well-behaved dragon by far,
And today he is bringing
this big wish for you
As only a really nice dragon
can do!

HAPPY BIRTHDAY
WITH LOVE

A Declaration by the Representatives of the UNITED STATES OF AMERICA, In General Congress assembled.

When in the course of human events it becomes necessary for [one] people to dissolve the political bands which have connected them with another, and to assume among the powers of the earth the separate and equal station to which the laws of nature & of nature's god entitle them, a decent respect to the opinions of mankind requires that they should declare the causes which impel them to the separation.

We hold these truths to be self-evident; that all men are created equal, that from that equal creation they derive rights inherent & inalienable, among which are the preservation of life, & liberty, & the pursuit of happiness; that to secure these ends, governments are instituted among men, deriving their just powers from the consent of the governed; that whenever any form of government becomes destructive of these ends, it is the right of the people to alter or to abolish it, & to institute new government, laying it's foundation on

The unanimous Declaration of the thirteen united States of America.

THE TEN EDITING SKILLS

1	Taking stock of a manuscript
2	Cutting what's not needed
3	Adding missing material
4	Improving order
5	Checking facts
6	Improving word choice
7	Improving sentences
8	Catching spelling mistakes
9	Checking punctuation
10	Preparing the final manuscript

EDITOR'S MARKS

1	~~eat~~ or ⌿	delete (cut)
2	∧	add a missing letter or word
3	↻	move
4	¶	paragraph
5	∨̇	add an apostrophe
6	⊙	add a period
7	⌄	add a comma
8	∨ ∨	add quotation marks
9	sp	check spelling
10	#	space

ANSWERS

Caution! Editing is not an exact science. Two editors working on the same material may change it in very different ways. Therefore, when discussing the worksheets in class, be open to different answers. Students, of course, should be asked to explain or defend the answers they come up with.

Worksheet 1. What's Good and What Could Be Better?

Answers will vary. Some parts of the amusement park that will seem fine to most students are: free trips to the moon, 2¢ burgers, first-aid doctor on duty at all times, free rock concerts, and fireworks every night.

Parts that might need changing are: the gap in the roller coaster track, the $25.00 charge for cold drinks, the air-polluting smokestack, the sign that says the park is closed *every day*, and the shark in the swimming pool.

Worksheet 2. Making Changes in a Piece of Writing

1. line 4 2. lines 1, 8, and 9 3. their, wasn't, of 4. line 10 5. line 6 6. line 9 7. line 1

Worksheet 3. Extra! Extra! Do Something About It!

The clock has an extra hand. The barber's door has two handles. The car has two steering wheels. The traffic light has two or three extra lights. The juggler has an extra hand. There are two stop signs. One stop sign has an extra *stop*. The dog has two tails. The man walking the dog has two hats on. The litter sign has an extra *litter*. The word *school* has an extra *o*.

Worksheet 4. Cutting Extra Words

A. sing B. the, in C. in Kentucky, D. permitted, E. the F. the G. will H. a, it, on I. the or a, clam

Worksheet 5. Cutting Sentences That Don't Belong

A. Florida is famous for its oranges. B. Many people enjoy going to boxing matches. C. This happened in June. D. There are skyscrapers in many cities.

Worksheet 6. Cutting Extra Steps

A. Step 1 B. Step 3 C. Step 5 D. Step 3

Worksheet 7. What's Missing

The door has no doorknob. The teacher's desk is missing a leg. The ABC's over the chalkboard is missing the letter T. The clock has no hands. The clock is missing the number 5. The flag is missing the stars. The "Good Morning" message on the board is missing the *M*. The bird cage has no bars. One student is sitting at a desk that isn't there. The elephant in the poster has no trunk. The book a student is reading has no words. The student who is standing has no shoes.

Worksheet 8. Missing Words

A. an B. is C. said D. the E. to F. a G. on H. a I. the, the J. egg

Worksheet 9. Completing Directions

B. Step 2. Break an egg into the pan.
C. Step 2. Dial the number.
D. Step 3. Take the photographs.

Worksheet 10. Adding Details to a Description

A. The triangle is inside a circle. B. A capital T is inside the circle. C. Inside the smaller square is a 4.
D. The word star is inside the circle.

Worksheet 11. Where Does It Belong?

A. On the clock, reverse the 3 and 4.
B. In the alphabet, reverse the *M* and *N*.
C. The caboose should come at the end of the train.
D. On the phone, reverse buttons 1 and 8. Also reverse 6 and 7.
E. Reverse the postage stamp and the return address.

Worksheet 12. First Things First

(The order of events in the story may vary.) 1. The balloon is pumped up. 2. The boy sails upward. 3. The bird flies toward the balloon. 4. The balloon pops. 5. The boy gestures for help. 6. The boy yells for help. 7. The girl pumps up another balloon. 8. The boy lands on the new balloon. 9. The boy thanks the girl.

Worksheet 13. Word Moving

A. You are going to catch a big mouse. B. You'll have many happy cat naps. C. You will chase a dog up a tree. D. You will star in a TV cat food commercial. E. Someday you'll turn into a lion. F. You will never have another flea bite in your life. G. You will always land on your feet. H. Your owner won't mind if you scratch the furniture.

Worksheet 14. Tangled Directions

A. Step 3 should be Step 2. B. Step 2 should be Step 1. C. Step 5 should be Step 1.

Worksheet 15. What's Wrong?

The stop sign is round, not eight sided. The stripes on the flag go in the wrong direction. The car is going the wrong way on the one-way street. The batter in the ball game is standing where the pitcher belongs. The batter is gripping the wrong end of the bat. The pitcher is standing in the batter's box. The ball in the pitcher's hand is shaped like a cube. The outfielder is facing out rather than in. In the market, the sign reading "oranges" is over the bananas. The speed limit reads "350 Miles Per Hour." A "No Parking" sign is posed next to a parking meter. The man in the car is facing the wrong way.

Worksheet 16. Finding the Facts

1. Einstein died in 1955. 2. The U.N. first met in 1946. 3. The Nile River is 4,157 miles long. 4. Queen Elizabeth I was born in 1558. 5. Cleveland, Ohio, was named for Moses Cleaveland. 6. The Spanish flag has no stars on it. 7. A worker bee usually can live weeks or months. 8. The Wright brothers' first flight was December 17.

Worksheet 17. Yummytown

1. Answers will vary. Here is one way to go.
   A. Go north on Second Avenue to M Street.
   B. Turn west.
   C. Go to Fifth Avenue.
2. Answers will vary. Here's one possibility.
   A. Go east on Q Street.
   B. When you come to the Taco Store, turn north. This will be Third Avenue.
   C. Head north three blocks and you'll be there.

Worksheet 18. Nice Is Not Nice Enough

Answers will vary.

Worksheet 19. Don't Always Say Said

Answers will vary.

Worksheet 20. Don't Go Wrong with Go!

Answers will vary. Here are some possibilities.
A. sail B. gallop C. fly D. slither E. swing F. dive G. climb H. soar I. stomp J. march K. shoot

Worksheet 21. The Thing Problem

Answers will vary.
A. pen B. word C. clipper or scissors D. meter E. knob F. bat or ball G. umbrella or raincoat H. telescope or binoculars

Worksheet 22. One Word Can Be Better Than Two

Answers will vary.
A. strolled B. whispered C. gripped or grasped D. moaned or whimpered E. jumped F. tugged or jerked G. slammed H. banging or pounding I. shouted or screamed J. gulped K. chased L. raced M. whispered

Worksheet 23. Spaghetti Sentences
Answers may vary.
A. The most common last name in the U.S. is Smith. The most popular first name is William.
B. How big is your heart? It's about the same size as your fist.
C. Americans seem to like peanuts. The average American will eat 200 pounds of this food in a life-time.
D. Have you seen bumps on your tongue? They're your taste buds.

Worksheet 24. Actor and Action
A. is B. gathers C. are D. feeds E. look F. wear G. is

Worksheet 25. Stand-In Words
A. it B. They C. it D. them E. it F. them, their G. their H. them

Worksheet 26. One Plus One Equals One
Answers will vary.
A. Because I'm hungry, I'll eat. B. It rained today, but it didn't rain yesterday. C. When my cat ran away, the mice came out to play. D. Although I'm not very brave, still I like scary movies. E. I like football and baseball, but I don't enjoy fishing. F. First my shoelace broke and then my bike had a flat tire. G. Because I had no money, I could not go to the circus.

Worksheet 27. Seller Spellers
Low-Cost Market, Party Favors, Carpet Care, Power Vitamins, Flavor Right Soda, No Decay Tooth-paste, Fast Photo Service, Open All Night, Kids' Clothes, Shoe Shine Polish, Easy Shine Soap Pow-der, Save and Shave Razors

Worksheet 28. License Plates
Zooming, Stop and Go, Dog Lover, Hello, My Car, Travel, Slow, Quick, Ready to Go

Worksheet 29. Silly Headlines
A. House. B. Shop C. Car D. Dogs E. Tooth F. Stocks G. Taxes H. Flood I. Storm J. Bell

Worksheet 30. Ridding Riddles of Spelling Mistakes
A. your B. so C. great D. a E. when F. break G. for H. not I. banana

Worksheet 31. Double-Checking Your Spelling
A. of B. they're C. funny, Can't D. (no errors) E. it's, to, buildings F. (no errors) G. and, break H. your I. whole J. happy

Worksheet 32. All's Well That Ends Well
Answers will vary.
A. ? B. . or ! C. . D. ? E. . or ! F. . G. ! H. ? I. . J. . or !

Worksheet 33. Commas, Commas, Commas
The answers appear on the bottom half of the worksheet.

Worksheet 34. Run-On Words
A. You will lead a happy life.
B. What you lost you will find.
C. Good luck is yours forever.
D. You will be rich and famous.
E. for the   Hope for the best.
F. The sun will shine   The sun will shine on you.
G. dream will   Your favorite dream will come true.
H. You will have many friends   You will have many friends.

Giving Readers a Break

Writers usually break their books into chapters. This makes the books easier to read. The same trick works when you write a short paper. If you break it into parts called *paragraphs*, it will be easier to read.

You can tell where a paragraph begins because the first word is moved a little to the right. This is called *indenting*. In this paragraph the word *You* is indented.

Sometimes writers forget to break a piece of writing into paragraphs. Later, they go back and use this sign — ¶ — to mark the places where paragraphs should start.

1. On your own paper, rewrite the following joke in four paragraphs. The editing marks tell you where each paragraph should begin.

A man was having dinner in a restaurant. When his bowl of soup came, he seemed angry. "Is something wrong, sir?" asked the waiter. "There certainly is!" said the man. "There's a fly in my soup." "Don't worry," smiled the waiter. "The heat will kill that bug in a few seconds."

2. Read the following joke. It should be written in five paragraphs. Your job is to use the paragraph mark — ¶ — to show where each paragraph should start. Once you've marked the joke, copy it onto another piece of paper.

"Something odd happened last night," said my friend. "What's that?" I asked. "I snored so loud I woke myself up," my friend replied. "What did you do about your problem?" I wanted to know. "Nothing to it," said my friend. "I just got up and went to sleep in the next room."

Putting Words into People's Mouths

The words that characters say in a story is called *dialogue*. It's set off from the other words by quotation marks: " ". These marks come in pairs — they go at the beginning of a speech and at the end.

When a speech has two parts, each part must have its own pair of quotation marks. Here's an example:

"It's time," I said, "to go."

Put in the missing quotation marks from the following joke. Use this editor's mark: ∀.

The Duck's Bill

One day a hungry duck came into a restaurant and sat down at the counter.

I'll have tuna on white bread, he said, but no pickles, please.

The owner brought the sandwich.

Very good, said the duck when he finished. It's just the way I like it.

The owner, thinking the duck wouldn't know much about money, wrote out a bill for fifteen dollars. The duck was shocked but, not liking to argue, paid the money and got up to leave.

You know, said the owner, you're the first duck we've ever had in this restaurant.

I'm not surprised, replied the duck. At the prices you charge, you won't be getting many others, I can promise you.

Editing Captions

The following captions have many problems. Read them carefully and you'll find spelling mistakes, fact mistakes, extra words, missing words, and so on. Mark up each caption using the editing marks that you've learned. Then write a new copy of the caption.

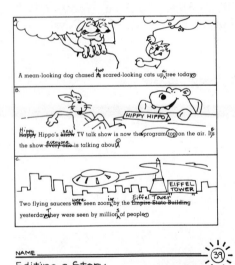

A mean-looking dog chased two scared-looking cats up tree today.

Happy Hippo's new TV talk show is now the program top on the air. It's the show everyone is talking about.

Two flying saucers were seen zoom in by the Empire State Building Eiffel Tower yesterday they were seen by million of people.

Editing a Letter

Letters that you write to your friends need as much careful editing as your school papers.

Here's a chance to practice. Use the editing marks you've learned to correct the many problems in the following letter. You may need to use a dictionary.

When you're done, copy the letter neatly. Be careful not to make any new mistakes.

145 Madison Place

New York, New York 10016

March 19, 1933

Dear Mom,

I want you to know that I've arrived safe and sound in New York City. This is an interesting place to be. There are million of people here, but I haven't found any big apes like myself yet. People here do get upset easily. For example, yesterday I was out taking a walk and I accidentally knocked down a few building. Everyone was yelling and screaming within a few seconds, police drove up in cars with sirens on top that made loud noises. To get away from all of that, I climbed up a tall skyscraper called "The Empire State Building. It gives you an amazing view of the whole city.

That's it for now.

Love,

Kong

Editing a Story

The following table needs lots of editing. If you read it carefully, you'll find extra words, missing words, misspelled words, missing punctuation, wrong punctuation, unclear words, run-on words, run-on sentences, and other problems, too.

Your job is to use the editing marks you've learned to improve this story. When you're done, copy the story neatly on another piece of paper.

The Fox and the Crow

The fox was out for a walk one day when he saw the crow sitting on a branch of a tree. In the crow's mouth was a piece of yummy-looking cheese. The cheese made the fox hungry. "I'd sure like a bite of that cheese," he said. "Would you like to share it with me?" The crow shook her head and kept her beak shut tight on the cheese. The fox thought for a while and then said, "I'm not really interested in the cheese," he said. "I came looking for you because I wanted to hear your wonderful voice. Would you sing for me?" The crow was so pleased to hear these words that she began a song. But no sooner had she opened her mouth than the cheese fell down, right onto the fox's tongue. As he swallowed the treat he said, "Here's some advice in return for the cheese. Don't be fooled by flattery."